*"The way I look at it is I'm paid insane amounts of money to make different faces and tell lies, pretending to be someone else."*

# JOHNNY DEPP

## *A Retrospective*

## Steven Daly

INSIGHT  EDITIONS

*San Rafael, California*

*To Georgia Catherine Daly*

INSIGHT
EDITIONS

PO Box 3088
San Rafael, CA 94912
www.insighteditions.com

www.INSIGHTEDITIONS.com
FOR WEB EXCLUSIVE CONTENT!

Find us on Facebook: www.facebook.com/InsightEditions

Follow us on Twitter: @insighteditions

First published in the United States in 2013 by Insight Editions.

Originally produced in Great Britain in 2013 by Palazzo Editions.
Text © 2013 Steven Daly
Publisher: Colin Webb
Design: Bernard Higton
Editorial: Judy Barratt / James Hodgson
Picture research: Emma O'Neill
Please see picture credits on page 286 for image copyright information.

Library of Congress Cataloging-in-Publication Data available.

ISBN: 978-1-60887-259-6

ROOTS of PEACE    REPLANTED PAPER

Insight Editions, in association with Roots of Peace, will plant two trees
for each tree used in the manufacturing of this book. Roots of Peace is an
internationally renowned humanitarian organization dedicated to
eradicating land mines worldwide and converting war-torn lands into
productive farms and wildlife habitats. Roots of Peace will plant
two million fruit and nut trees in Afghanistan and provide farmers there
with the skills and support necessary for sustainable land use.

Printed and bound in China by Imago.

10 9 8 7 6 5 4 3 2 1

---

Opening page: The view from here. Portrait by Christophe d'Yvoire, March 1994.
Title page: Photocall for *Sweeney Todd: The Demon Barber of Fleet Street*, London, November 2007.
Page 7: Arriving at the Venice Lido to present the Golden Lion for Lifetime Achievement to Tim Burton,
Venice Film Festival, September 2007.
Page 9: Portrait by Armando Gallo, Hollywood, June 2006.

# Contents

Do I search out the weirdest thing I can find, and then do it, just because it is the weirdest thing I can find? Well, the answer is no. I just do the things that I like. However, I have to admit that what I like does tend to be left-field."

"*All the amazing people that I've worked with—Marlon Brando, Al Pacino, Dustin Hoffman—have told me consistently: Don't compromise. Do your work, and if what you're giving is not what they want, you have to be prepared to walk away.*"

# Introduction

**S**everal years back, Johnny Depp's longtime collaborator Tim Burton famously called his sidekick "a character actor in a leading man's body." The description is so trenchant that it's tempting to suggest that a Johnny Depp book containing just those eight words alongside a photographic history of the actor's career would be a respectable undertaking. Hopefully, however, there is something more to be gleaned from this retrospective of Depp's cinematic works.

So what can one hope to learn about Johnny Depp? It's fair to say that we have never seen Depp's like before—this is a film star who has repeatedly shown himself capable of turning mainstream films into global blockbusters, but who still seems unwilling to use these hit movies as career building blocks in any conventional manner. Whatever one thinks of Johnny Depp professionally or personally, it's virtually impossible to imagine him giving a second thought to the kind of cynical strategizing that sees so many actors methodically trading off big-budget roles with parts in worthy independent projects.

> *"There's a drive in me that won't allow me to do certain things that are easy. I can weigh all the options, but there's always one thing that goes, 'Johnny, this is the one.' And it's always the most difficult, always the one that will cause the most trouble."*

Head gear—bandanas, hats, and designer glasses have been the essence of Depp style since his days as a teen heart-throb in *21 Jump Street* (opposite).

Right: Older and wiser, but still determined. At the Royal World Premiere of *Alice in Wonderland*, February 2010, London.

Any other actor blessed with Depp's Apollonian looks would likely have set his sights on trying to become the next Paul Newman, an archetypal mantle that only a handful of today's male stars could even aspire to. But each of the potential contenders is burdened with at least one disqualifying characteristic: George Clooney? Looks the part, but too knowing. Ryan Gosling? A peerless young actor who lacks the iconic presence of a genuine movie star—not that he's likely to lose any sleep over that. Matt Damon? Too "everyman." Brad Pitt? A heavyweight talent smothered by tabloid attention. Johnny Depp, on the other hand, seems to earn "Best Actor of His Generation" plaudits whenever he takes on a serious dramatic role—but he seems equally engaged by the challenge of giving new life to Captain Jack Sparrow, the fey and cowardly "hero" of *Pirates of the Caribbean*.

Even though Depp turns 50 this year, there is still something of the teenager about him: a distinct sense that he chooses projects according to how much fun he'll have making them, and—in many cases—how much confusion they will cause among his followers, and the countless media experts who are paid to impose a rational pattern on the "choices" made by stars of Depp's wattage.

Searching for some long-term pattern within Depp's body of work is a fairly thankless task; perhaps because of the haphazard manner in which he entered the movie industry, he seems positively to revel in the random, picking out his projects with the proverbial whim of iron. Which is just as likely to lead to a questionable re-make like Tim Burton's *Charlie and the Chocolate Factory* as it is to Depp's arresting dual-character cameo in *Before Night Falls*, the 2000 feature directed by epicurean art-world superstar Julian Schnabel.

Over the years Depp has refined his ability to give extremely congenial interviews that reveal exactly as much as he wants them to reveal, and no more. I discovered this particular aptitude when I profiled him for *Vanity Fair* magazine in 2004. The functional nature of our meeting militated against

*"I remember feeling a freak when I was about five. I looked at other kids and had weird feelings about being the odd one out."*

Depp's collection of tattoos has steadily grown over the years. One of the first designs incorporated his mother's name, Betty Sue.

any earth-shattering revelations being delivered, but it wasn't until afterwards that I realized I'd just had my pocket picked, metaphorically speaking. Although the interview went well, and the resulting article was fairly satisfactory, right after talking to him I felt as though I'd come away with more top-drawer quotes than actually existed on my tape.

What I got was a variation on the standard Johnny Depp interview, which is still a good deal more edifying than the standard interview given by most of his contemporaries. He talked about what his attitude to acting was after he accidentally wandered into that profession: "I figured I'll keep doing it until they say 'No.'" When talking about the type of celebrity he acquired through the teen-cop TV series *21 Jump Street*, Depp tellingly used a musical analogy that must have sounded quaint to most of his younger admirers. "I thought to myself, Is this Kajagoogoo? Is it A-Ha? Because it sure ain't The Clash, it ain't Iggy, and it ain't Bowie. I knew it was wrong—it was a lie."

Depp also discussed the aftermath of an interview he gave to a German magazine the year before, in which he was quoted as calling his native US a "dumb puppy" in comparison to older nations on the other side of the Atlantic. Although Depp maintained that his printed quotes were not accurate, he had still been so eager to correct the impression they made that he actually called several individuals who were offended by them, and painstakingly explained himself. "If you still feel like I'm a shithead or a schmuck afterwards, then fine. But at least hear me out."

If this should lead anyone to assume that Johnny Depp is too literal-minded or slow-witted to appreciate irony, it has to be said that this is not the case. Depp is an astute individual who fully understands the lingua franca of our times; but unlike the vast majority of his peers he simply chooses not to let such considerations affect his work. For instance, it wouldn't have taken a genius to work out that *The Tourist*, the ill-advised 2010 spy romp that Depp made with Angelina Jolie, was just a raised eyebrow away from being camp—but he opted not to raise his eyebrow. As always he played it straight, placing his trust in the director and the script. While this may have been the wrong

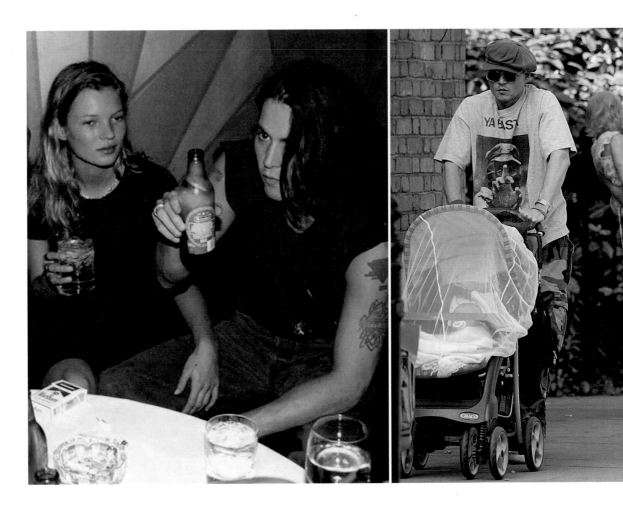

approach, one gets the sense that Depp is one actor who would rather be wrong than take the easy option.

In terms of analyzing Johnny Depp, *The Tourist*—a substandard film by anyone's reckoning—is instructive in another regard. While he was making the movie in Venice, Depp got an up-close look at the kind of media pressure his co-star Jolie and her husband Brad Pitt have to live with; afterwards Depp commented that he'd "probably be in prison" if he was subjected to similar levels of attention, and given his track record he may have been only half-joking. Depp's most notorious tabloid moments came when he spent a night in the cells after trashing a New York hotel room in 1994 and when he threatened paparazzi photographers in London in 1999. Further unwelcome publicity came when River Phoenix tragically collapsed and died outside Depp's club, the Viper Room, in 1993.

While a lot of ink was expended on these incidents, Depp has for the last decade or so enjoyed an existence that is surprisingly low key for a movie star in the $50 million-per-picture bracket.

This state of affairs was engendered partly by the actor's $3.6 million purchase of a Caribbean island in 2004, and partly by the fact that his other main domicile during his long-running relationship (officially ended in June 2012) with the French actress Vanessa Paradis was a remote villa in the south of France. However, neither of these locations is in itself terminally prohibitive to tabloid lenses; Depp has somehow accrued a critical amount of *respect* even among media professionals who would sneer at anyone who uttered that word in public.

All of which makes it even more difficult to get a bead on the true nature of this singular entertainer. When it comes to Johnny Depp, one finds oneself looking beyond all the standard-issue interviews and seeking scraps of revealing information wherever they can be found. When I interviewed him in 2004, lest I seem like a stalker (which I am not—honestly) I refrained from telling him that I had previously interrogated several of his old girlfriends, as well as the mother of his two children: namely, Sherilyn Fenn, Winona Ryder, Kate Moss, and Vanessa Paradis. Only Moss was actually going out with Depp when we spoke,

and as it turned out she offered a modicum of insight without being prompted by a single invasive question.

The year was 1996, and *The Face* magazine had assigned me to write a cover story on the English model, who was then in the middle of a four-year relationship with Depp. When the lunch interview was over I happened to mention that I'd seen recently several copies of an out-of-print Iggy Pop autobiography in a downtown store about a mile from the Greenwich Village restaurant where we met. Although it was raining that afternoon, Moss insisted that we walk to the store: Depp had been informally educating the 22 year old on all things classically underground, from Iggy to William Burroughs to Jack Kerouac and beyond, and she wanted to get him a copy of the book as a token of her appreciation. The vision of Depp as one of the counterculture's last surviving True Believers was reinforced eight years later when I got a chance to ask him about his early cultural influences; most of these he had found through his older brother Daniel, who was born in 1953. The thought of Johnny Depp as a bastion of Baby Boomer values goes some

> *"I still feel like I'm this 17-year-old gas-station attendant in South Florida, and that it's other people who place this strange stigma on you."*

way toward explaining his approach to acting—but it still leaves more than enough questions unanswered.

A slightly more orthodox source of salient Depp data would be *Movieline* magazine's May 1990 cover story on the actor, who had just been named "Male Star of Tomorrow" in a Las Vegas ceremony thrown by the National Association of Theater Owners. The *Movieline* piece caught Depp at a particularly significant juncture in his career, when he was a 26-year-old striver emerging into the limelight from relative obscurity—this was shortly before the release of *Cry-Baby* and *Edward Scissorhands*, at a time when the actor was fully aware that the media were waiting for him to prove himself as a contender worthy of serious consideration.

As far as many observers were concerned, one mark against Depp at that point—aside from his *21 Jump Street* teen-idol fame—was his track record with women. He was sporting a $75 tattoo of the words "WINONA FOREVER" (famously changed, in later years, to "WINO FOREVER"). The ink had

been applied in tribute to his then-fiancée Winona Ryder; their engagement, along with Depp's own career, was just slightly devalued by the fact that he had also become betrothed to two of his previous girlfriends, the actresses Jennifer Grey and Sherilyn Fenn.

*Movieline* writer Stephen Rebello wondered—in retrospect, poignantly—if Depp was "more than merely another of the [James] Dean pretenders of the Michael Parks, Christopher Jones, or Maxwell Caulfield variety?" Depp showed admirable self-awareness in this 1990 interview, frankly discussing his earlier bouts with drugs and alcohol and expressing mild disbelief at the letters he was getting from teenage fans. "I'm just as fucked up as the next guy," he averred.

Depp has never quite seemed at ease within an industry so antithetical to his deeply ingrained rock value system, but in 1990 he expressed that unease in a manner that film-business bible *Variety* might term "unprofesh." He showed open disdain for *21 Jump Street*, and talked about counting down the days left on his highly lucrative contract with the show's producers.

*"I think that it's important to want to surprise the audience, to want to surprise yourself, and I think that it's important, each time out of the gate, to go, 'This may be the one where I lose big. This may be the one where it's too much or not enough.' I think that it's important as an actor."*

Depp had already registered his discontent by, among other things, burning his underwear on the *21 Jump Street* set, but in the *Movieline* interview he insisted on playing the victim card as well. In an outburst that must make him cringe now, Depp blamed his plight on "people in ties with very big pens and hulking desks who do bad things to you."

Within a few years Johnny Depp would learn to be more guarded, and to express himself in more charming, self-deprecating ways. Depp has often referred to himself as "franchise boy" in the wake of the *Pirates of the Caribbean* films, each of which has earned hundreds of millions of dollars at the worldwide box office. Since Depp is the key factor in the success of the *Pirates* franchise, he was able to command over $50 million for the fourth film in the series—and even more for the fifth.

On its face, the very notion of starring in a movie based on a Disney theme-park ride seemed preposterous at best when it was initially announced. And then there was the prospect of Johnny Depp deciding to star in the kind of movie you could watch on a plane without having to pay for headphones. What could possibly have enticed the world's coolest actor to take on such a project? If Depp had a dollar for every time that question had been asked throughout his career, he'd be almost as rich as he is today, as a universally beloved actor whose films have collectively grossed more than $7.5 billion worldwide.

At this point it remains to be seen whether Captain Jack Sparrow can recapture the popular imagination at a fifth time of asking, but it's hard to imagine Depp losing any sleep over that question. For the first time he seems to have found some semblance of a road map for his career, which now seems to involve alternating the *Pirates* films with Tim Burton projects, then filling in the blanks at will.

Perhaps the final word here should be left to Johnny Depp himself. In that 1990 *Movieline* interview, Depp showed a certain perspicacity when he was asked to predict the way in which he would ultimately be remembered. "Johnny Depp got his big break in *21 Jump Street*," said the future megastar. "He went into films, then went on to be a Las Vegas entertainer."

I don't have a deep strategy about which films I want to make. But I refuse to do any movie that would make me want to throw up. That eliminates every dumb action movie, cop movie, or anything where people get blown up or shot every five minutes. I don't want to sound like some elitist who only does 'serious' stuff, but I like to think I'm making films that actually say something about the world instead of simply trying to make a profit."

# The Movies

# The Early Years

*A Nightmare on Elm Street* (1984)
to *Cry-Baby* (1990)

································································

"I'd never acted before. I'd never done school plays. Nothing. The fact that it was totally new to me was a tremendous challenge."

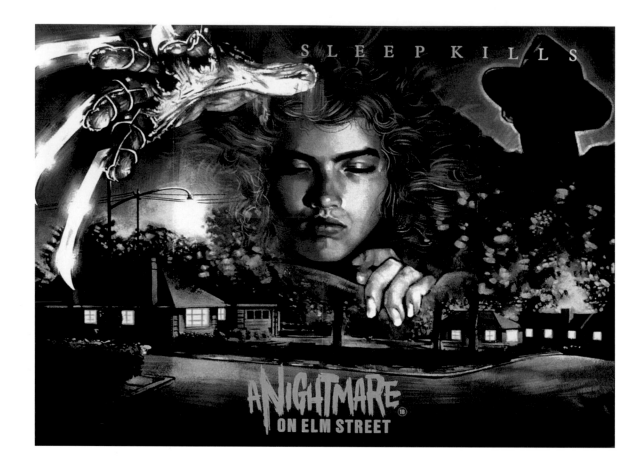

SLEEP KILLS

A NIGHTMARE ON ELM STREET

t wasn't until 1983 that Johnny Depp, aged 20, began to shift his focus—casually at first—from rock 'n' roll to acting. Depp's first wife, makeup artist Lori Anne Allison, to whom he was married from 1983 until 1985, introduced him to one of her former boyfriends, Nicolas Cage. The quixotic young actor seems to have recognized Depp as a kindred spirit, because he urged the Florida arriviste to consider acting as a career, rather than music. Despite Depp's dearth of experience in (or aspirations toward) the dramatic arts, Cage's agent got him a meeting with the casting agent Annette Benson, who secured him an audition with the horror-movie auteur Wes Craven.

Craven was in the process of casting the first of his *Nightmare on Elm Street* movies, and Depp was up for the part of an ill-fated frat-boy type named Glen Lantz. Although the lank-haired novice looked nothing like the character described in Craven's script, the director was sufficiently impressed to give him the part. (According to one, possibly apocryphal story, Craven's 16-year-old daughter ran lines with Depp before the audition and may have had some influence over her father's decision.)

*"I made some shitty movies when I was starting out, but I'm not embarrassed by them, especially as I didn't think I was going to be an actor—I was just trying to make some money. I was still a musician."*

Bergman it ain't: the poster for 1985 teen romp *Private Resort*.

Throughout his acting career, Depp has always espoused a fairly low opinion of his own abilities, but thankfully Wes Craven saw something in him at that first audition. "Johnny was more worldly than all the pretty boys coming in," the director recalled. "He chain-smoked and had these yellow fingers. He was more worldly somehow."

*A Nightmare on Elm Street* introduced a generation of young moviegoers to the talon-gloved, lava-skinned arch-villain Freddy Krueger, the nemesis of Depp's character. In keeping with horror-movie protocol, Depp disregards his girlfriend's desperate imprecations to *avoid falling asleep at all costs*—the moment he dozes off he finds himself getting violently sucked down into his bed, after which the entire bedroom becomes engulfed in blood.

*Nightmare* may have been Wes Craven's latest box-office smash, but Johnny Depp was quite aware that the film's success owed precious little to his own presence in it. In fact he later admitted that, "after that movie came out I never thought that there would be others. I didn't necessarily want there to be."

But of course there were; even if they'd occasionally justify Depp's initial apathy about the movie business.

Depp's next film, the 1985 teen comedy *Private Resort*, was a far remove from Wes Craven territory—but most young actors with an ounce of self-respect would have found it as frightening as any horror movie. The film—which features Depp's first nude scene, and saw him starring alongside fellow newcomer Rob Morrow—was shot at an actual Florida resort, and was so lacking in depth that the swimming pools looked positively oceanic by comparison. *Private Resort*'s bathrobe-tight plot mainly involved two young buddies lusting after a series of big-haired, curvaceous, and unattainable females. In other words this was a picture that fitted in perfectly with the countless other movies that defined the eighties as the decade when Hollywood discovered how much money could be made just by pandering lazily to a teen male demographic.

Although Depp would probably prefer that his résumé was not besmirched by the words *Private Resort*, at the time he simply shrugged the movie off as a bit of "basic filthiness."

*"I was this product. Teen boy. Poster stuff. All that stuff that I wasn't."*

From eye-candy to "can-do": As he took his profession increasingly seriously through the eighties, Depp worked hard to transcend his poster-boy image.

As far as Johnny Depp was concerned, movies were still far less significant than rock 'n' roll.

Then again, despite the paddling-pool prurience of *Private Resort*, Depp began to give more thought to this new profession he'd stumbled into. "When I saw how bad I was, I decided I better do something about it," he told *Movieline* magazine in 1990. Depp signed up for acting lessons at the Loft Studio in Los Angeles, and read all the classic instructional books by Uta Hagen, Stella Adler, Stanislavski, et al.

Among the neighbors in Depp's apartment building were members of a local band named Rock City Angels, who'd periodically try to enlist him as their new guitarist. He politely turned down these overtures. After hitting a dead end with The Kids, Depp had gotten a couple of decent breaks in the movies, but even those had led to just a handful of one-off TV gigs; he was still living a financially insecure existence in Los Angeles, and certainly didn't see another rock band as the answer to his problems.

There had been just one offer of a regular acting paycheck, from the producers of a new Fox TV cop series called *21 Jump Street*, a piece of hokum about a squad of fresh-faced police officers who go undercover in high schools to investigate various crimes. Even though Depp regarded the show as a piece of fluff, its producers weren't taking no for an answer. So after realistically weighing up his options, Depp accepted the role of baby-faced cop Tom Hanson, a decision that would guarantee him a salary of $45,000 per episode and oblige him to spend most of his time on location in Vancouver, Canada.

The year before Depp headed off to the wilds of British Columbia, his career had taken one more of those arbitrary turns that would continue to shape his acting résumé over the coming decades. Right out of the blue, iconoclastic director Oliver Stone handed Depp a small but not insignificant role in the Vietnam War film *Platoon*, which starred a handful of well-established and highly regarded young actors. In acting terms, Johnny Depp would have to learn quickly how to stay afloat in

Depp's appearance in Oliver Stone's *Platoon* gave him the kind of credibility that he could not get from *21 Jump Street*. Although Private Lerner was only a minor role, Depp would end up outranking the film's stars, Willem Dafoe, Charlie Sheen, and Tom Berenger (opposite).

the deep end. Not only was Stone's new movie infinitely more prestigious than Depp's random selection of other projects, it also presented the challenge of working for almost two months in the jungles of the Philippines. Depp must have been among the few crew members who had not, up to that point, ventured beyond the borders of his native United States.

Oliver Stone spoke with giddy enthusiasm about his young discovery, avowing that he could tell "from a mile away" that Depp was destined to be a major Hollywood star. The grizzled and sybaritic Vietnam veteran felt certain that this kid Depp was an "original," and in his moments on screen in *Platoon* the accidental actor sustained this intriguing thought.

Depp's *Platoon* character, Private Lerner, did not join his comrades in the kind of recreational gunplay and locker-room badinage that characterizes Stone's movie. As the platoon's translator, Lerner empathizes with the Vietnamese civilians who tell him that they've been forced to let the Vietcong take over their village, so they can use it as a base from which to

launch attacks on US forces. Lerner pleads with his alpha-male colleagues on the locals' behalf in an attempt to prevent a My Lai-style massacre of innocents. The soldiers nonetheless torch the village and shoot a female civilian; meanwhile Lerner attempts to evacuate the local children. As the platoon forges its way deeper into the oppressively dense Vietnamese jungle, it is ambushed by Vietcong forces. Depp's character is wounded in the firefight, then saved by a fellow soldier. We last see him being evacuated in a helicopter that is packed with other wounded

"*I gotta tell you, man, it was highly emotional. You put 30 guys in the jungle and leave them there to stay together for two weeks, just like a real platoon, and you build a real tightness. It's almost like a family. We became a military unit, a platoon.*"

and dead servicemen. While Depp's role didn't call for any scenery-chewing bravado, and he was more or less completely overlooked by *Platoon*'s reviewers, he was beginning to establish the kind of quietly authoritative on-screen presence that has become his trademark.

Despite his modest amount of big-screen exposure, Depp was to enjoy (or, as he might have put it, endure) a high level of public recognition thanks to his role in *21 Jump Street*, a series he detested with a passion, even though he was getting a reported 10,000 fan letters a month. Whenever he was on location in Vancouver, Depp felt like he was missing out on the kind of action he really wanted. The band he'd declined to join, the Rock City Angels, had gone and got themselves one of the biggest major-label deals that anyone could remember. (They went on to be dropped after just one unsuccessful album.) And even though Depp had just had the privilege of working with a world-class movie director, his exile in Canada denied

him the opportunity to trade in that credential for respectable roles that might help him establish a solid reputation within the industry. But his immediate future belonged to *21 Jump Street* and the Fox Network, which was only interested in getting Depp's face on the covers of teenybop magazines.

Every time Depp complained to the media about how *Jump Street* was making him feel like an indentured servant, he unintentionally revealed to the industry how much of a novice he was. If the networks didn't insist that every actor on all their new series must sign multi-year deals, the ensuing chaos would practically put these companies out of business. The regular drip of stories about Depp's petulant on-set behavior—as well as the underwear-burning incident, he also refused to appear in certain episodes—did little to dispel the growing suspicion that this handsome kid from Florida may not be quite as worldly as Wes Craven had surmised back in 1984.

If there was one movie director with a keen sense of the inherent absurdities of teen celebrity it was Baltimore's John

Waters, the man whom William Burroughs dubbed "The Pope of Trash" on the basis of the transgressive, low-budget cult movies he made in his home town during the sixties and seventies. The perpetually frustrated star of 21 *Jump Street* had spoken of his desire to "work with an outlaw" and, when he heard that John Waters wanted to meet him, he felt like his prayers had been answered. By this point, however, Waters' original maverick spirit had become diluted, to say the very least; and besides, where on earth was Depp going to find an actual "outlaw" who could afford his $1 million per-movie salary? ($1 million was probably more than the combined cost of all the trashy, Baltimore-based films that had made John Waters' name.)

By the late eighties Waters had been adopted as Hollywood's in-house freak, and in 1988 he was given $2 million to spend on making *Hairspray*, a bright and kitschy film about an early-sixties TV dance show—the picture turned a healthy profit, and was sufficiently inoffensive to be adapted into a long-running stage musical. John Waters' follow-up movie was to

be *Cry-Baby*, another story derived from distant memories of adolescent life in Baltimore. This movie, set in the decade before *Hairspray*, was a spoof on the juvenile delinquent pictures of the fifties, and the kind of airbrushed "rock 'n' roll" musicals that Elvis Presley used to make by the truckload, films that became unbearably bland after he left the US Army in 1960. Using terminology that was already somewhat outmoded in 1990, Waters referred to his latest vision as "King Creole on acid."

As always, the new film showed Waters' adroitness at the art of stunt-casting: Among his hand-picked troupe of audience-pleasing human punchlines was ex-porn star Traci Lords, reformed "revolutionary" heiress Patricia Hearst, former Warhol "superstar" Joe Dallesandro, and superannuated beefcake idol Troy Donahue; plus the "godfather of punk," Iggy Pop, a hero of Depp's who would later become a good friend. Casting the film's title character, a handsome and brooding juvenile delinquent who's named after his unique ability to shed a single tear at will, was a more serious matter, however. The 42-year-old Waters

With maverick director John Waters at the wheel and Johnny Depp in the saddle, *Cry-Baby* was a kitsch parody of 1950s rock 'n' roll musicals. The movie brought the up-and-coming actor to the critics' attention and was to be the first of many starring roles. In the back seat is Traci Lords as Wanda Woodward (right).

bought a bushel of teenybop magazines, and only had to pore over them briefly before he found the ace face that he was after. That matinee-idol visage gazed out at him from the covers of most of these publications—it was a kid called Johnny Depp, whom Waters enthusiastically dubbed "the best-looking gas-station attendant who ever lived." This was the only actor John Waters wanted to see in the *Cry-Baby* role. As it turned out Depp could hardly have wished for a better opportunity at this awkward juncture in his budding career.

*Cry-Baby*'s budget of $12 million may have been chicken feed by the standards of mainstream Hollywood, but this level of funding was something John Waters would

barely even have dreamed about just a couple of years before. It was a sum that would allow him to recreate every detail of the quaint era he was spoofing.

Waters—who went on to make a cameo appearance on *21 Jump Street* in February 1990 as a character named Mr. Bean—may have been satirizing an era that had long ago been drained of any comedic potential, but that didn't stop Johnny Depp from grasping the golden opportunity to showcase another facet of his acting abilities while wickedly mocking the teen-idol crown that Fox TV had thrust upon him.

Depp's character, Wade "Cry-Baby" Walker, is the leader of a *West Side Story*-esque gang called the Drapes, and a periodic resident at "juvie hall." (Beneath the leather,

Wade apparently has the heart of an all-round entertainer, because during one spell of incarceration he organizes an in-house dance troupe.) Back in his "Pope of Trash" days, Waters barely paid lip service to the notion of storytelling, preferring arbitrarily to combine oddball-character vignettes with random scenes included mainly for their shock value. But now that he was making $12-million movies, the dapper, pencil-thin director was obliged to tie them together with an actual plot. *Cry-Baby* was consequently garnished with a variation on the old Romeo and Juliet theme, with Depp's moody malcontent attempting to recapture the heart of the intermittently errant good girl Allison Vernon-Williams (Amy Locane).

We need not concern ourselves with the particulars of the turbulent courtship at the center of *Cry-Baby* (John Waters certainly didn't!), because if this film was "about" anything, it was about Johnny Depp. The 26 year old instinctively understood the imperative of playing it straight as the John

Waters circus raged around him, and proved that he had the acting chops to do so. Few other actors of Depp's generation could have sustained Wade Walker's incongruous stoicism throughout Waters' camp comedy without sneaking at least one conspiratorial wink at the audience, just to show that they "got it." Johnny Depp's *Cry-Baby* performance therefore brought to mind a passing remark by Wes Craven about the young actor having an "old soul."

Which is not to say Depp's *Cry-Baby* role demanded two hours of deadpan passivity. At one point in the film he performs a rockabilly number on stage, conjuring up the white-trash conviction and sultry demeanor that was once synonymous with the pre-Army Elvis Presley. (Depp lip-synchs during this scene; many years later, in *Sweeney Todd*, he found a project that showcased his more-than-adequate singing voice.)

When the music stops, Wade rips open his shirt to reveal a tattoo of an electric chair on his chest, inked in honor of his late

"King Creole on acid." The spirit of Elvis is channeled through the young star.

Overleaf: Portrait by Philip Saltonstall, circa 1987.

*"There were people who thought* Cry-Baby *was a bad idea. But I've always admired people like John Waters, who never compromise. The easy way is boring to me."*

parents. He earnestly informs the audience that, "electricity killed my mommy and daddy." If you could point to one moment when John Christopher Depp officially became "Johnny Depp," this would surely be it. With just one film he had managed to shed the stigma of *21 Jump Street* and connect with an entirely new audience, redefining himself as a rising star with the kind of on-screen presence that people might actually pay to see. Depp would continue to refine that presence, which didn't really conform to any of the pre-existing archetypes. Perhaps it's enough to say that, with the possible exception of Paul Newman, there isn't another male movie star who could attribute their career to the elusive and seemingly natural virtue of being, for want of a better term, "ironically handsome."

Only in retrospect can one suggest that Johnny Depp's *Cry-Baby* performance was one of his defining moments as an actor. At the time, no one knew whether he was just a TV star who got lucky; starring in a John Waters film isn't the kind of thing

that would have given Depp, or his agents, a burning sense of conviction about which of the predefined young-actor career paths he should follow. The 1990 profile of Depp in *Movieline* magazine posed an astute question regarding the actor's post-*Cry-Baby* prospects: "Should an incipient sex-god do self-parody before his time?"

Well, at least the critics had finally taken notice of Depp. Even though most of them were disappointed with John Waters' soft-serve product, the film was a financial success and Depp's performance was singled out for a good deal of acclaim. For instance, David Denby of *New York* magazine called Depp "a very shrewd, sensual performer" and, in concurrence with Oliver Stone, Wes Craven, and John Waters, predicted that he could become a big movie star. Depp would, of course, ultimately reach that exalted plateau, but to say that he got there using the proverbial "road less traveled" would be a considerable understatement.

*"I decided early on to be patient and wait for the roles that interested me, not the roles that would advance my career. I never wanted to be remembered for being a star."*

# Edward Scissorhands

1990

"I love Edward.
He was total honesty.
Honesty is what
matters, and I have an
absurd fascination
with it."

*"I didn't know Tim very well. He rehearsed everybody, the whole cast, except me. He didn't rehearse me. I think he was trying to keep me separate from everyone. It was good for me and it was good for the film."*

Tim Burton, Vincent Price, and Johnny Depp in the Gothic surroundings of the Inventor's castle, from which Edward is coaxed by kindly Tupperware saleswoman Peg Boggs. *Edward Scissorhands* was the first of eight collaborations to date between Depp and Burton.

After the spiritual high-colonic that was John Waters' *Cry-Baby*, Johnny Depp moved on to work with a maverick director of a different stripe; a man who would give Depp the most important role of his career and who'd end up, in the eyes of the moviegoing public, almost umbilically connected to the actor. The auteur in question is, of course, Tim Burton, whom Depp first encountered at an April 1989 meeting at the Bel Age Hotel in Los Angeles. The director had seen Depp on *21 Jump Street*, but the actor knew very little about the man who'd just created the global marketing juggernaut known as *Batman*. Nonetheless, the two of them apparently hit it off instantly, going on to forge the kind of long-term working relationship that's rarely seen in modern-day Hollywood.

In his foreword to the Tim Burton interview compendium *Burton on Burton*, Depp explains that "Tim need do nothing more than… look at me in a certain way, and I know what he wants from the scene." In the same section he talks about

his initial reaction to the version of the *Edward Scissorhands* screenplay he got from his agent in late 1989. "I read the script instantly and wept like a newborn," wrote Depp. But not only did it take a great deal of time and effort to finally get a *Scissorhands* script to Depp's door; at one point it looked as though that same script might end up languishing in a drawer indefinitely.

Tim Burton made his directorial debut in 1985 with *Pee-wee's Big Adventure*, a mildly surreal comedy based on a successful kids' TV series that was known for keeping adult viewers amused with regular hints of camp and sexual innuendo; the movie adaptation of *Pee-wee*—starring Paul Reubens as the titular, bow-tied man-child—was shot for only $6 million, and went on to earn $40 million domestically for Warner Bros. Burton's follow-up film, *Beetlejuice*, another Warner production, turned a modest budget of $15 million into $75 million worth of business at the US box office. Even so, when this young director, a former Disney animator, was put at the helm of Warner's $35 million

Having crafted a magical topiary garden for his castle, Edward revels in his new-found skills as a dog groomer with lonely housewife Joyce (Kathy Baker).

revival of its long-dormant *Batman* franchise, he began work on the project with dozens of skeptical voices echoing around the soundstage. *Batman* went on to be an international blockbuster, hauling in over $400 million worldwide, a phenomenal figure that made the film Warner's biggest-ever hit, and ensconced Burton within Hollywood's A-list talent pool.

Despite his proven ability alchemically to transform Warner's money into giant mountains of currency, the company wasn't too receptive when Burton declared that his next film would be an esoteric project entitled *Edward Scissorhands*, a modern-day fairy tale he'd originally conceived decades before. "It's an old story," he later admitted. "It's *Frankenstein*, it's *Phantom of the Opera*, it's *King Kong*."

For some reason, Warner's top executives decided to pass on this relatively inexpensive proposition, and let their golden boy stroll right off the studio lot. Undaunted, the director formed his own company, Tim Burton Productions, with Denise

Di Novi, best known as a principal producer on one of the most influential teen comedies of recent decades, *Heathers*.

Tim Burton personally hired the novelist Caroline Thompson to write the script for *Edward Scissorhands*, initially showing her just a few of his old sketches of the title character. Remarkably enough, Thompson wanted to use the images as her sole reference point for her screenplay. The writer's first draft was uncannily true to Burton's vision for the project, incorporating all the ideas he wanted the movie to convey.

When it came time to cast the film's crucial title role, Burton's first choice was Johnny Depp. "Tim believed in me," the actor recalled. "He rescued me from being a loser, an outcast, just another piece of expendable Hollywood meat."

However, Burton and Di Novi's newly formed company still lacked the cash to start production on *Edward Scissorhands*—to the filmmakers' relief Twentieth Century Fox stepped in to provide the remainder of the movie's $20 million budget.

*"This role was freedom. Freedom to create, learn, experiment and exorcise something in me."*

Filming began in a suburban Florida town, where Burton had dozens of tract houses painted in pastel colors in a broad parody of Burbank, California, the dull suburban enclave in which he was raised.

*Edward Scissorhands* opens with Winona Ryder, made up to look like an old lady, telling a bedtime story to one of her grandchildren. It's the tale of a scientifically engineered youngster who lives alone above the aforementioned pastel wasteland in an utterly incongruous Gothic castle. One evening Edward's solitude is disturbed by a visit from a struggling Tupperware saleswoman named Peg Boggs (Dianne Wiest). Mrs. Boggs instantly forgets about her plastic wares when the castle door opens to reveal an astonishing vision: Johnny Depp dressed in a punk-ish carapace of black leather, with a heavily scarred, kabuki-white visage, and razor-sharp shears where his fingers should be.

Peg instinctively takes pity on this otherworldly being, the creation of a mad scientist (horror-movie icon Vincent Price), who died before he could complete his work by giving the boy real fingers. After admiring Edward's breathtaking topiary garden, Mrs. Boggs insists on coaxing him out of his isolation and down to the "normal" suburban world below.

Thanks to Peg's benevolent guidance, Edward becomes accepted into the local community, whose members are in awe of his topiary skills; and even more impressed when he reveals his talent for cutting the hair of the local women and their dogs. No one minds that Edward's interactions with the local populace invariably end up in mutual incomprehension. Throughout the picture, Depp (who has fewer than 200 words of dialogue in the whole film) evinces the wide-eyed grace of a silent movie star, a quality that was central to the subsequent, dramatic rise in his professional standing, and his instant election into the pantheon of Hollywood's most promising

Before long, Edward discovers that not all his friends in the "normal" world are as faithful as this one, and he retreats to his former home.

young stars. (Depp's confidence received a tremendous boost during the filming of *Edward Scissorhands* when he got a call confirming that he'd finally been freed from his onerous *21 Jump Street* obligations.)

Despite Edward's abundance of guileless charm, there are still a handful of townsfolk who continue to view him with suspicion, particularly when he enters into a relationship with Peg Boggs' daughter Kim (played by Winona Ryder, Depp's real-life girlfriend at the time). Kim's previous boyfriend goes into a jealous rage, and when he frames Edward for a robbery the movie—or the grandmother's bedtime story—takes an ugly turn.

Virtually every member of the community turns against Edward and—despite their lack of traditional pitchforks and torches—they chase him back to his lofty domicile, where he must continue to live in splendid isolation. Tim Burton's "old story" resonated deeply with audiences worldwide, and *Edward Scissorhands* managed to rack up a formidable box-office take of $86 million.

The film's pre-publicity focused almost entirely on directorial wunderkind Tim Burton, but after its release it was Johnny Depp who found himself besieged by the mass media. As far as the public was concerned, Depp's deft and touching portrayal of Edward Scissorhands had revealed a startling new dimension to the former *21 Jump Street* star; he had now established himself as a bona fide movie star, and earned a level of goodwill that would make him practically bulletproof for years to come.

"He had this unconditional love. He was this totally pure, completely open character, the sweetest thing in the world, whose appearance is incredibly dangerous— until you get a look at his eyes. I missed Edward when I was done. I really miss him."

Depp and Winona Ryder were already an item by the time they acted opposite each other in *Edward Scissorhands*, their four-year relationship having started in 1989.

# Arizona Dream

1993

"Everything has
been done ten zillion
times and if you
can, at least, try for
something a little
different, then
why not?"

*"I was thrilled to work with Kusturica because I saw* Time of the Gypsies *and it was one of the greatest things I've ever seen."*

In *Arizona Dream*, Depp plays fish-obsessed Axel Blackmar. Landing this role enabled him to observe close up the respected Bosnian director Emir Kusturica (left).

In the early nineties, still bathed in the warm glow of his *Edward Scissorhands* triumph, Johnny Depp embarked on a two-year stretch in which he made three fanciful movies of scant consequence. Had the actor continued down that petal-strewn path for much longer, he might as well have gotten himself a large tattoo of the word "QUIRKY" right above the infamous "WINO[NA] FOREVER" script. This was a period that suggested a seriously flawed sensibility at work, but as always Depp would somehow manage to recover his equilibrium, pull a rabbit out of the hat and keep moving forward on his seemingly uncharted course.

The first of the three strenuously whimsical movies Depp made in the early nineties was *Arizona Dream*, a logic-warping fever-dream that was filmed by the esteemed Bosnian director Emir Kusturica. One might be tempted to call Kusturica's undertaking "quixotic" if it didn't make Cervantes' fabled misadventurer look eminently sensible in comparison.

Kusturica's strong international reputation was well deserved, and the Eastern European also happened to possess an uncanny ability to connect with judges at major film festivals. In 1985 he won the Palme d'Or at Cannes with *When Father Was Away on Business*, a family drama set in 1950s Yugoslavia; in 1989 the festival's judges handed Kusturica "best director" honors for his third film, *Time of the Gypsies*; and he would later go on

to earn a second Palme d'Or in 1995 for *Underground*, his epic three-hour history of post-War Yugoslavia.

While every one of the aforementioned projects is estimable in its own right, not one of them has anything whatsoever to do with the United States—so it was somewhat surprising to find that when the director proposed to create what sounded like a fairly nebulous interpretation of the "American Dream" and its attendant iconography, a group of French investors thought it prudent to bankroll him to the tune of some $17 million. Then again, during this period Kusturica must have absorbed a decent measure of US culture during his stint as a lecturer at New York's Columbia University. In fact the idea that inspired *Arizona Dream*—originally titled *The Arrowtooth Waltz*—came from one of his students, David Atkins, who ended up getting sole credit for the film's screenplay.

So what is the idea behind *Arizona Dream*? That's the question that had critics desperately scrambling for disparate interpretations of the film upon its belated US release in 1994. Some prominent reviewers simply went for the easy option: file under "magical realism." The *New York Times*' Janet Maslin called the film a "slapstick psychodrama with a heavy dash of magical realism," while Kevin Thomas of the *Los Angeles Times* described Kusturica's vision as a "dazzling, daring slice of cockamamie tragicomic Americana envisioned with magic

realism." (For all the confusion it created, it should be noted that *Arizona Dream* had its fair share of supporters among America's leading movie critics.)

The key to understanding Kusturica's allegorical grab bag remains equally elusive two decades after the fact; which would hardly come as a surprise to anyone who'd read the dreamy ruminations the director offered up about his first movie project in the New World. The director revealed that among his central preoccupations about the United States was the fact that it "was always the country of cars and movies." So far, so vague.

Johnny Depp's *Arizona Dream* character is a 20-ish orphan named Axel Blackmar, whose first scene is suggestive of—to use the parlance of the time—a slacker with mystical predilections. Blackmar is a lowly functionary employed by the New York Department of Fish and Game, for whom he tags and releases fish—*or does he*? "Most people think I count fish, but I don't," Axel explains. "I listen to their dreams." Thus the tone is set.

The movie's "inciting event"—as they say in Hollywood screenwriting seminars—comes when a menacing dreamer named Paul (Vincent Gallo) cajoles Blackmar, with the help of a handgun, to fly out to Arizona to be best man at the wedding of Axel's car-dealer uncle Leo Sweetie. (Leo is played by Jerry Lewis, in his first significant big-screen appearance since 1983 when he starred in *The King of Comedy*, Martin Scorsese's bleak comedy-drama classic.)

It's only when Axel arrives in Arizona that the true nature of this singular movie starts to reveal itself: which is to say, Kusturica presents us with a parade of central characters so doggedly eccentric that at times Johnny Depp's solid presence seems to be the only thing that stops *Arizona Dream* from simply floating away. For instance, Jerry Lewis—as the uncle who gives the ethereal Axel Blackmar a job in his Cadillac dealership—often appears to think that he is acting in one of the early-sixties comedies he made alongside Dean Martin.

OVERSIZE LOAD

Meanwhile, Faye Dunaway (soon to co-star with Depp in *Don Juan DeMarco*) plays a wealthy former mine-owner named Elaine Stalker, whose heart is set on building and flying in her very own Wright Brothers-style aircraft. Axel assists Elaine in this definitively quirky venture, and in the process encounters her desire for his youthful form.

Elaine Stalker's daughter Grace is essayed by the dependably unnerving Lili Taylor, adding to her collection of mentally unstable young women with a *sui generis* oddball who plays accordion music (usually "Besame Mucho") to her pet turtles when she isn't also pining after Axel. During one particularly uncomfortable dinner scene, Grace's unrequited crush on the handsome stranger puts mother and daughter at each other's throats.

*Arizona Dream* took almost a year to complete, because in early 1992—just a few weeks into production—Emir Kusturica suffered what sounds not unlike a nervous breakdown. Some

reports attributed this to his heavy workload; however, the more credible explanation is that the director felt unable to carry on working after he heard that Bosnian Serb forces were about to lay siege to Sarajevo. (Ominously enough, even as the film had entered its pre-production phase, the Bosnian war was breaking out.)

Kusturica's absence from the set of *Arizona Dream* prompted the movie's financiers to consider hiring a replacement director. Showing the kind of solidarity that is not frequently seen in the movie industry, the cast unanimously dismissed this idea, and vowed to wait as long as it took for the director to get back behind the camera. After a three-month interregnum Kusturica resumed production and completed *Arizona Dream*, which ends by revisiting one of its recurring motifs: a dream sequence in which Johnny Depp has visions of Eskimos, huskies, sleds, Alaska, and freshly caught halibut. Depp and Jerry Lewis enact a scene that could almost fit into a vintage Lewis/Dean Martin

Axel helps eccentric would-be aviator Elaine Stalker (Faye Dunaway) to realize her ambitions. When the director had to take time out from filming, the movie itself was left up in the air.

comedy: Dressed as Eskimos, they babble away at each other in a vague approximation of the Inuit language. (In certain versions of the film, subtitles reveal that they are in fact engaged in philosophical discourse.)

It would hardly be fair to judge a film like *Arizona Dream* by the usual financial criteria, as it was released sporadically in international territories, and only played in three cinemas in the US two years after its initial European release. As a large number of French cinéastes still regard Jerry Lewis as something of a demigod, it is known that the film did quite well in that country. However, it would be safe to say that there are few people outside of France who'd claim that Kusturica's

personal take on the American Dream was entirely satisfactory on any level. Then again *Arizona Dream* did earn the director a Special Jury Prize at the 1993 Berlin International Film Festival.

*Arizona Dream* was not released in the UK until the summer of 1995, at which time some promotional engagements were fulfilled by Vincent Gallo, even though he was only a member of the movie's supporting cast. Gallo is a perverse and outspoken veteran of New York's 1970s punk scene who, as a middle-aged hipster, has become known for volubly expressing extreme right-wing political views (and who released a song entitled "I Wrote this Song for the Girl Paris Hilton"). The solidarity that had been displayed by the cast during the film's production was apparently a thing of the past, because Gallo elected to break the traditional thespian code of honor by proffering, unprompted, an unusual analysis of his old acquaintance and *Arizona Dream* co-star Johnny Depp to a *Guardian* interviewer. (The journalist in question, incidentally, declared *Arizona Dream* to be a "masterpiece.")

According to Gallo, "The tragedy of Johnny Depp is that the exterior—the TV pop star-turned-bad-boy-waif-lover-hipster-friend-of-Jim-Jarmusch—is totally uninteresting... If he would only allow himself to be who he really is, somebody who's traumatized and trapped by his childhood and emotional life, then he would be interesting, a great person, a great talent. He is one of the most funny, talented, likable, sweet, authentic people I've ever met."

# Benny & Joon

1993

......................

"I enjoyed the
slapstick part of
the movie, although
I sustained some
injuries."

Depp plays Sam, an eccentric loner with an obsession for silent movies who develops a relationship with the unstable Joon.

"*I had such a great time rediscovering Keaton, Chaplin, and Harold Lloyd. Comedy, especially when it is so physical, is extremely demanding. I developed an even greater respect for those guys as I began to try to do what they had accomplished in such a seemingly effortless way.*"

**D**epp's next film, *Benny & Joon*, was another slice of would-be Americana helmed by a foreign national. In this case the director could at least claim to hail from the American continent: Jeremiah Chechik, a Canadian, is a former director of TV advertisements whose one credential within the US film industry was directing the hit 1989 comedy romp *National Lampoon's Christmas Vacation*, a hefty hunk of American cheese.

The original story for *Benny & Joon* was jointly conceived (with associate producer Lesley McNeil) by a former circus clown named Barry Berman, who penned the screenplay himself. Despite its unusual provenance, when Berman's script was picked up by Metro-Goldwyn-Mayer it was regarded in Hollywood as something of a hot property, with Tom Hanks and Julia Roberts, and Tim Robbins and Susan Sarandon being among the names mentioned as potential participants. Ultimately Johnny Depp and Mary Stuart Masterson signed on

to *Benny & Joon* to replace the actors who were originally cast in two of the film's principal roles, Woody Harrelson and Laura Dern. The latter pair reportedly quit the project for similar reasons, with both actors deciding to take on parts in much bigger movies.

Masterson played Joon and the role of her garage-owning, solid-citizen brother Benny went to the redoubtable Aidan Quinn. Depp played a character named Sam, who ends up having a profound impact on the lives of both siblings, Joon's in particular.

One of the things that drew Depp to *Benny & Joon* was Sam's fixation with the icons of silent comedy, chief among them Charlie Chaplin, Harold Lloyd, and Buster Keaton. Depp had a similar reverence for these actors, and before filming began he spent over a month studying hundreds of hours of silent films, and training with Dan Kamin, choreographer on the 1992 biopic *Chaplin*. Just in case anyone was about to miss Depp's many visual homages to the silent-movie era—and Keaton in particular—Chechik shows Sam reading a book called *The Look of Buster Keaton* as *Benny & Joon*'s credits roll.

Sam is a dyslexic, quiet-spoken loner who becomes romantically involved with Joon, a mentally unstable young woman whose whimsical affectations include sporting a scuba-diving suit as day-wear. Joon's less innocuous traits include a pyromaniac tendency that may or may not be responsible for the blaze that killed both her parents.

Sam does not expend many words in his courtship of Joon, preferring to win her over with various bits of comedic business

he's learned from his beloved silent movies. As is often the case, Depp gives the impression of being just slightly removed from the rest of the film, although his character does possess his own brand of fanciful behavior: In one scene we see him taking a bath, fully dressed.

As the romance between Sam and Joon continues to develop, it is obvious that any relationship built on such shaky foundations cannot produce the kind of happy ending that Hollywood executives so desperately crave. It is clear to Sam—and more so to Joon's brother Benny—that his girlfriend's behavior is more than just eccentric, and that this is someone who could never hope to sustain anything resembling a normal existence.

While he was acting in this romantic soufflé, Johnny Depp's mood was anything but light, because his relationship with Winona Ryder was beginning to fall apart. It was around this time that Depp started to make periodic references to his habit of "poisoning" or "medicating" himself to block out the unpleasant realities of real life. According to the actor,

Playing a Buster Keaton imitator enabled Depp to hone his visual comedy skills, and here reprising Chaplin's bread dance from *The Gold Rush*.

Both on and off screen, Depp's love life was in turmoil.

his medication mainly took the form of alcohol, but over the years there have been frequent, usually non-specific references to drug use in Depp's early adulthood. On a couple of the rare occasions on which he has discussed the subject in any kind of detail, he has revealed—according to one sensationalistic UK tabloid, at least—a passing affinity for opium (a substance so rare that one hardly ever hears it mentioned in modern times). The actor has more often spoken about cocaine, insisting that he despises its teeth-grinding payload of "synthetic happiness."

As enigmatic as Johnny Depp may appear, one of the few things about him that all his co-workers seem to have agreed on throughout his career is that he is among the most consistently professional A-list actors out there. Meaning that, whatever means he may have been using to medicate himself on the set of *Benny & Joon*, they did not impair the quality of his day-to-day work.

Despite its lack of a cheerful resolution, *Benny & Joon* generally enjoyed good reviews upon its release, performing respectably at the box office. Meanwhile, Johnny Depp enjoyed the personal bonus of being nominated for a Golden Globe for the Best Performance by an Actor in a Motion Picture (Comedy/Musical). Well, it's hard to say if "enjoyed" is the right word—because it would still be some time before Depp got either his professional or romantic life back on track, which meant that the "self-medicating period" was far from over.

WHAT'S
EATING
Gilbert
Grape?

# What's Eating Gilbert Grape

1993

"Gilbert would seem like a pretty normal kind of guy, but I was interested in what was going on underneath, in the hostility and the rage that he has."

Left: Clockwise from left, Laura Harrington, Johnny Depp, Juliette Lewis, Darlene Cates, Mary Kate Schellhardt, and Leonardo DiCaprio.

The third and final part of Johnny Depp's "small-town trilogy" was *What's Eating Gilbert Grape*—and if the actor imagined that he'd found a groove with these three successive works, to most people in the outside world that groove was starting to look suspiciously like a rut. *Gilbert Grape* had several elements in common with Depp's previous two films: a foreign director, mentally impaired characters, and lashings of eccentric "local color"; more pertinently, all three movies featured Depp in passive roles.

Depp had spoken out for years about consciously avoiding the kind of predictable leading-man roles that would normally be standard issue for any actor with his combination of looks and ability—but in choosing to work on the margins and play so many undynamic characters, Hollywood's former "one to watch" was in danger of falling into another, equally predictable stereotype, albeit at the opposite end of the acting spectrum. Having said that, Depp could always be relied upon to stamp his authority on any film, no matter how slight the basic material,

"I understand the feeling of being stuck in a place whether it's geographical or emotional. I can understand the rage of wanting to completely escape it and from everybody and everything you know and start a new life."

In the absence of his father, Gilbert supports his mother Bonnie (Darlene Cates), above, and his younger brother Arnie (Leonardo DiCaprio), far right, while finding time to develop a romance with free spirit Becky (Juliette Lewis), center.

and he managed to endow several harebrained projects with levels of respectability they scarcely deserved.

*Gilbert Grape*—which by no means belongs to the latter category of films—is based on a novel of the same name, written by Peter Hedges, who also wrote the screenplay. Hedges' book was picked up for adaptation by Lasse Hallström, the Swedish director who made his breakthrough film, *My Life as a Dog*, in his Scandinavian homeland in 1985 before debuting in America six years later with the mildly underwhelming romantic comedy *Once Around*.

Hallström was fortunate enough to number among his *Gilbert Grape* cast two of the outstanding young actors of the time, Johnny Depp and the 18-year-old Leonardo DiCaprio, who first established himself as a serious contender with the 1993 family psychodrama *This Boy's Life*. In *Gilbert Grape* DiCaprio plays Johnny Depp's younger brother, who suffers from an unnamed mental affliction that bears some resemblance to autism. The boys' mother, Bonnie, is played by Darlene Cates, a 500-pound

non-actor whom Peter Hedges discovered while watching an episode of *The Sally Jessy Raphael Show* on the subject of obesity. Fortunately for everyone concerned, Cates graces Hallström's film with a touching, naturalistic performance.

*Gilbert Grape* was filmed between February and April of 1993 at locations in Austin, Texas, that could pass for the fictional small town of Endora, a place where nothing much ever happens. For Depp's character, "nothing much" involves a life working at a grocery store to support his immobile mother (whom he compares to a "beached whale") and his younger brother, whose strange compulsion to keep climbing a local water tower ends up getting him arrested. Gilbert's entropic existence is shaken up by the arrival of a strange young girl named Becky (played by the 19-year-old supernova actress Juliette Lewis), who engages him in a love affair when she briefly becomes stranded in Endora.

The romantic interlude with Becky has a galvanizing effect on Gilbert, judging by his response to his mother's

Overleaf: Portrait by Albert Sanchez for
*Movieline*'s *Hollywood Life*, November 1992.

not-unexpected death toward the end of the movie. After Gilbert overhears officials griping about the onerous task of removing Mrs. Grape's oversized corpse from the family residence, he diligently removes every item of value from the house before calmly transforming it into an improvised funeral pyre.

Judging by reports from the *Gilbert Grape* set, Depp's state of mind was not significantly brighter than that of his character. The actor's largely long-distance relationship with Winona Ryder was plainly entering its terminal phase, a situation that sent Depp into further bouts of "self-medication." Once again, though, he seemed able to severely abuse his body without diminishing his own high professional standards.

One person on the set who became fascinated with the Depp enigma was writer Peter Hedges, who noted that Depp, in his professional life, had "an almost burning desire to make ugly choices." Director Lasse Hallström had his own angle on the actor playing Gilbert Grape, although we may never know exactly what the Swede had in mind when he said, "[Depp]

belongs somewhere better. He has real ambitions, but he is deeply afraid of being considered pretentious."

Leonardo DiCaprio's *Gilbert Grape* performance secured him nominations in the best supporting actor category for both the Golden Globes and the Oscars—further evidence for the widely held suspicion that the compilers of such shortlists will always favor any actor whose character suffers from some form of disability. Looking beyond such predictable observations, *Gilbert Grape* served to highlight a telling distinction between Depp and DiCaprio, who has since built his career by methodically sticking mainly to "high end," prestigious fare and working with the most solidly established collaborators. You can be certain that Johnny Depp is as aware as anyone that there have been moments in his own career when he could have taken a similar path to DiCaprio's, but if Depp has any regrets about following his own instincts, anyone who could conceal such doubts so well over such a long period would deserve to be anointed "Best Actor of His Generation."

*"Success is a strange word, y'know.*
*It started making me feel even more*
*freakish, even more weird."*

# Ed Wood

1994

......................

"I wanted to make him extremely optimistic, innocent and a brilliant showman all at the same time."

As has often been the case with Tim Burton, he did not arrive at his next collaboration with Johnny Depp by a direct route. Before Burton made his fanciful movie biography of "the world's worst filmmaker," Ed Wood, for Walt Disney, the *Edward Scissorhands* auteur was slated to direct the picture for Columbia Pictures along with a more prestigious Columbia project, *Mary Reilly*, which would present a new take on the well-worn story of Dr. Jekyll and Mr. Hyde. The film was adapted from a novel in which the good/evil twosome were observed through the eyes of Dr. Jekyll's housekeeper, a part that Burton had earmarked for Johnny Depp's former inamorata, Winona Ryder. After developing *Mary Reilly* for two years, Burton ended up clashing with Columbia, which had decided to minimize its financial exposure by handing the title role to Julia Roberts, the quintessential mainstream movie star (aka "America's Sweetheart"). To add insult to injury, the company stridently refused to let Burton film *Ed Wood* in black and white,

Above: "Wow, I'm in!" Depp needed no persuading to team up with Tim Burton for the second time.

Opposite: Another satisfactory take for the "world's worst filmmaker."

or to grant him the level of creative control he felt that he had earned through his consistent success at the box office. The director, who suspected that Columbia had taken on *Ed Wood* only in order to secure his services on *Mary Reilly*, abruptly walked away.

Just one month before shooting was due to start, *Ed Wood* was immediately put into "turnaround," meaning that pre-production was halted, and the property was made available to any company that agreed to repay Columbia's investment in

the project to that point. As it transpired, virtually every major studio was eager to adopt the *Ed Wood* project, and work with one of the most commercially successful young directors of the period; but the film ended up at Burton's first employer Disney, under the aegis of its Touchstone division, which matched Columbia's budget of $18 million.

The life story of Ed Wood was suggested to Burton as the potential subject for a movie by a friend, director Michael Lehmann (*Heathers*, *Hudson Hawk*). Lehmann had been turned on to the idea by a pair of fellow USC film-school graduates, Scott Alexander and Larry Karaszewski, who had—improbably enough—written the first two *Problem Child* comedies. While Ed Wood's slender body of work was amateurish beyond belief, the cross-dressing former Marine (who enlisted right after Pearl Harbor and attained the rank of Corporal) had latterly accrued something of a cult following among the film-snob crowd; this was largely due to *Nightmare of Ecstasy*, Rudolph Grey's 1992 oral history of Wood's life, which Burton reportedly

"*This is a homage.
A real weird homage,
but nevertheless,
a respectful one.*"

Once he agreed to play
washed-up horror-movie idol
Bela Lugosi, Martin Landau
threw himself into the role
with a dedication that would
earn him an Academy Award.

optioned for $250,000. The groundwork for the Wood revival had been laid by a 1980 bad-movie compendium that cited the late director's *Plan 9 from Outer Space* (1959) as the official "worst movie ever made."

Tim Burton initially intended to take only a producer's role on the Wood movie, with Michael Lehmann directing; however, the project revived in Burton memories of seeing Wood's slipshod creations on television as an impressionable youngster in Burbank, and his growing affinity for the movie's subject spurred him on to direct *Ed Wood*, with Lehmann producing. "Who knows, I could become Ed Wood tomorrow," Burton once remarked.

During the six weeks in which Scott Alexander and Larry Karaszewski worked on their first draft of the *Ed Wood* script, Burton reached out to his erstwhile protégé/collaborator Johnny Depp to offer him the film's title role. "He said, 'There's no script,'" Depp recalled. "And I said, 'Wow, I'm in!'" Depp was

even more enthused when Burton related Ed Wood's life story to him; since the young actor had never before heard of this guy Wood, he contacted *Cry-Baby* director John Waters, who was only too happy to screen Ed Wood's greatest hits for his former leading man. Thus it was that, four years after *Edward Scissorhands*, the director responsible for *Plan 9 from Outer Space* would provide the second defining role in Depp's capricious Hollywood career.

Tim Burton had become fixated on the next part of the *Ed Wood* puzzle: to recruit a man some 35 years Depp's senior. Burton had decided that the veteran actor Martin Landau was the only person who could play the part of former horror-movie icon Bela Lugosi, whom Wood befriended and employed in Lugosi's twilight years, when he was living in obscurity with little more than a morphine habit to his name.

Landau was markedly less enthusiastic than Johnny Depp about signing on to Tim Burton's latest enterprise, mainly

Although by no means a blockbuster, *Ed Wood* cost 300 times more than its subject's most famous movie, *Plan 9 from Outer Space*.

because he felt that there was a complete lack of physical resemblance between himself and Lugosi. Burton asked Landau if he'd agree to let makeup artist Rick Baker try to overcome this hurdle. After working with Baker and shooting some test footage with Burton, Landau agreed to appear in *Ed Wood*; in order to capture Lugosi's distinctive modes of speech and movement, he immersed himself in the actor's old movies, showing an old-school sense of commitment that would ultimately pay off in spades.

Johnny Depp continued to cultivate his habit of modeling characters on at least one unlikely public figure; Depp felt that he had glimpsed something akin to Ed Wood's unhinged optimism during his *21 Jump Street* days, when he had attended an anti-drug event at the White House, and briefly met President Ronald Reagan. Tim Burton chipped in with some suggestions of his own, namely the Wizard of Oz, Mickey Rooney character Andy Hardy, and legendary radio personality

Casey Kasem. In the wake of his small-town trilogy, Depp described *Ed Wood* as a "breath of fresh air," and he put everything he had into re-creating Wood classics like *Glen or Glenda*, in which Wood plays both the male and female title roles. Later, in a *Film Threat* interview with the *Ed Wood* screenwriters Alexander and Karaszewski, Depp said, "It's the first time that I'm actually looking forward to seeing something that I was in... it felt like a really good departure from any of the other shit that I've done."

Depp's sly performance as Ed Wood—a man who never met a first take he didn't like—was the most accomplished of his career to that point. He devoutly resists any temptation to make so much as a single gesture or remark that might suggest to the viewer that Depp is somehow "in on the joke." While his Ed Wood may have worn a rictus grin throughout the entire duration of the film, neither he nor Tim Burton regarded their outlandish undertaking as any kind of joke. As the latter

"I was committed, completely committed. I was already familiar with Wood's films. I knew that nobody could tell his story better than Tim. Tim's passion became my passion."

Playing it straight: Depp's refusal to go for cheap laughs as the cross-dressing cinéaste resulted in a touching, respectful—and well-received—performance. Here with Sarah Jessica Parker (left) and Martin Landau (opposite).

Overleaf: At a party to promote *Ed Wood*, Cannes Film Festival, May 1995.

informed the *New York Times*, "There is something beautiful about somebody doing what they love to do, no matter how misguided, and remaining optimistic and upbeat against all odds."

As portrayed by Johnny Depp, Ed Wood maintains deranged positivity in the face of every conceivable setback, as well as a few that—despite being gleaned from a nonfiction book—simply beggar belief. Wood mouths silently along with his actors as they deliver his risible dialogue, cheerfully tolerates the most hazardous scenery ever seen on celluloid, and remains oblivious to the low-life elements who gravitate toward his sets. On a personal level, when Wood invites the ghoulish TV hostess Vampira (played by Burton's then-girlfriend Lisa Marie) out on a date, she responds by saying, "I thought you were a fag." Unfazed, Wood responds matter-of-factly, "No, no, I'm just a transvestite."

Burton and Depp manage to concoct a film that seems to float on a cloud of Wood's beloved angora, defining its own giddy realm outside the prosaic parameters of the biopic form. However, the heart of the piece is really the relationship between Wood and the ailing Lugosi, which allows Johnny Depp and Martin Landau to create some transcendent moments. Plus, there is the added bonus of Bill Murray sashaying across the

screen as Wood acolyte Bunny Breckinridge, who won't be happy until he finally has his sex-change operation.

Tim Burton cheerfully admits that verisimilitude was of little interest to him while creating *Ed Wood*. For instance, the film's young, clean-scrubbed supporting cast (including Patricia Arquette and Sarah Jessica Parker) in no way reflects the tawdry realities of Wood's real-life milieu. "I'm sure these people were more horrible than the way I'm portraying them," the director allowed; but "they've been made fun of their whole lives and I'm certainly not doing that to them." Burton does Wood the great favor of ending the film well before his subject entered a long decline that saw him making low rent porn, becoming an alcoholic, and dying in poverty in 1978, at the age of 54. As a further kindness, Burton includes a complexly manufactured scene in which Ed gets a stout pep talk from his idol Orson Welles.

On the eve of the film's release, one critic carped that *Ed Wood* was "destined to be the world's most expensive cult film." To which Tim Burton would surely have replied, "I know—isn't it great?" It's worth pausing here just to consider how much the film business has changed over the two subsequent decades, and how unlikely it would now be for a major studio to throw $18 million at a project of such marginal appeal.

Although *Ed Wood* performed poorly at the domestic box office, it did far better overseas, and the majority of the film's notices were laudatory, with Depp and Landau in particular receiving effusive acclaim. For connoisseurs of the Hollywood postmortem, there are a handful of obvious factors that likely explained the film's financial shortfall: Burton's insistence on shooting in monochrome, for instance, or the profound obscurity of his subject; not to mention the restrictive "R" rating that the movie was landed with. Strangely enough, the rating was applied not for any explicit kinkiness portrayed, but for Bela Lugosi's profane dialogue. At one point someone makes the mistake of mentioning his former rival Boris Karloff, and Bela explodes with rage, bellowing, "He isn't fit to smell my shit!"

Martin Landau went on to win his first Oscar for his performance in *Ed Wood*, with Rick Baker's makeup team being similarly honored. Tim Burton himself was not recognized by the Academy, and *Ed Wood* was one of his rare commercial failures; but these unfortunate facts did little to impede his growing stature as a director. Columbia, meanwhile, cast Julia Roberts in *Mary Reilly*, replacing Burton with the English director Stephen Frears. Made at a cost of nearly $50 million, *Mary Reilly* grossed approximately $12 million worldwide.

*The two things I inherited from my parents are insanity and chain-smoking."*

# Don Juan DeMarco

1994

..................

"The challenge for me
was creating a character
who is slightly cocky
and noble, but likable.
I needed to create
someone who has a
strong sense of himself,
but is still lost."

When novelist and screenwriter Jeremy Leven heard
that Johnny Depp was interested in playing the title
role in his directorial debut—originally to be called
*Don Juan and the Centerfold*—he thought all his prayers had
been answered. However, when word reached Leven that
Depp would agree to appear in the movie only if its producers
signed up Marlon Brando as his co-star, the aspiring director
must have felt as though he were the victim of some cruel
cosmic prank.

Brando, after all, was a semiretired septuagenarian at this
point, having acted in only four, unmemorable films since his
seismic performance as Colonel Kurtz in *Apocalypse Now* in 1979.
With each passing year, this former deity of American cinema
seemed to become more reclusive and—as suggested by his
post-1979 projects—eccentric.

Then again, as proved by Johnny Depp's desire to work with
him, Brando's iconic stature was hardly diminished by his latter-
day output. By pursuing the older actor relentlessly via phone and

mail, Depp played a significant part in pulling off the seemingly
impossible feat of roping Brando into a frothy romantic comedy
that was written and directed by a cinematic novice. (Depp later
joked, "I might go into casting now.")

Jeremy Leven's professional life prior to directing *Don Juan
DeMarco* involved stints as founder of a satirical off-Broadway
theater troupe, a low-level TV director, a novelist (with two movie
adaptations under his belt), as well as ongoing employment in
the field of clinical psychiatry. When New Line Cinema expressed
interest in adding *Don Juan DeMarco* to its production slate,
Leven insisted, somewhat hubristically, that he'd proceed only
if the company permitted him to direct the picture; presumably
it was Leven's modest stage and television experience that
convinced New Line to take a leap of faith and put him in charge
of its $25 million budget for the movie.

Leven said that the original inspiration behind *Don Juan
DeMarco* came from Lord Byron's early nineteenth-century epic
poem *Don Juan*, although by the time the script was completed

"Every woman is a mystery to be solved." Don Juan's remarkable story of harems and high romance is told through a series of flashbacks.

Marlon Brando    Johnny Depp    Faye Dunaway

Don Juan
DeMarco

NEW LINE CINEMA et FRANCIS FORD COPPOLA Présentent UNE PRODUCTION AMERICAN ZOETROPE UN FILM DE JEREMY LEVEN.
MARLON BRANDO. JOHNNY DEPP-Don Juan DeMarco. FAYE DUNAWAY RACHEL TICOTIN. BOB DISHY ET GERALDINE PAILHAS.
Casting LYNN KRESSEL. Musique MICHAEL KAMEN. Costumes KIRSTEN EVERBERG. Montage TONY GIBBS, A.C.E. Décors SHARON SEYMOUR.
Directeur de la photographie RALF BODE, A.S.C. Co-producteurs exécutifs ROBERT NEWMYER, BRIAN REILLY ET JEFFREY SILVER.
Producteurs exécutifs RUTH VITALE et MICHAEL DE LUCA. Produit par FRANCIS FORD COPPOLA, FRED FUCHS, PATRICK PALMER.
Écrit et réalisé par JEREMY LEVEN. © MCMXCV New Line Productions, Inc. Tous droits réservés Bande originale disponible chez A & M Records

Protesting his love for the sultry Doña Ana (Géraldine Pailhas).

it showed few traces of direct Byronic influence. The movie opens with a brisk example of Don Juan's irresistible seduction technique before suddenly taking on a dark tone. Depp's titular character is seen, in Zorro-esque drag, perched atop a tall billboard, with police officers and passers-by gawking up at him. This anachronistically clad 21 year old explains that he is none other than Don Juan—the mythical figure known for centuries as the "greatest lover in the world"—and that he wishes to die in a duel with Spain's greatest swordsman. Instead psychiatrist Jack Mickler (Brando) arrives on the scene to try to persuade this bizarre individual not to end his own life. Don Juan explains that he recently found his one true soulmate, only to lose her after divulging his prodigious sexual history.

Although Dr. Mickler (whom Don Juan insists on calling Don Octavio del Flores) is close to retirement he elects to take Don Juan on as a patient, for a 10-day period of evaluation that will determine whether or not Depp's character will be institutionalized indefinitely. Like the movie bank-robber who goes back to do "one last job," Mickler is obviously about to discover that things are never quite that straightforward. Don Juan outlines for Mickler, in a mellifluous Spanish accent, his unlikely personal origins, along with several of his more outrageous romantic exploits, which are shown in somewhat prosaic bodice-ripping flashbacks.

Rather than basing Don Juan on some unlikely public persona, or a combination of several such types—as was his habit—Depp elected to use an accent as the foundation for his character. He later admitted that he was particularly drawn to the suave cadences of Latino actor Ricardo Montalban, star of the kitschy and long-running TV series *Fantasy Island*. It was not, however, Depp's intention to imbue his performance with overt

camp component, and he engaged a Castilian voice coach to help him develop Don Juan's indomitable mode of verbal seduction.

In character terms, Marlon Brando finds himself somewhat short-changed, since much of Jack Mickler's dialogue tends to come in the form of standard-issue psychiatric observations. Brando is afforded more opportunity to shine—albeit not as brightly as he once did—in scenes that feature Mickler and his wife Marilyn, played by Faye Dunaway, whose taut features make a slightly alarming contrast with Brando's jowly visage. It turns out that Jack Mickler's sessions with the delusional romantic Don Juan end up reigniting the couple's stagnating marriage— a sentimentally portrayed state of affairs that Mickler might well describe as "transference." Thankfully it is the patient who comprehends this dynamic, describing it thus: "You need me for a transfusion, because your blood has turned to dust."

Given his character's outsized pathology, Depp's performance in *Don Juan DeMarco* is surprisingly restrained, perhaps due to his regard for Marlon Brando; however, it is Depp's consistency that holds the film together. At the end of Don Juan's 10-day observation period, Dr. Mickler has established his real name and background, and the reasons behind his adoption of the "greatest lover" persona. Don Juan drops the pretence to address a panel of Mickler's colleagues, and quietly delivers the statement that will, he hopes, save him from being institutionalized. This is the moment where Depp, with quiet authority, steps up and effectively takes possession of the whole enterprise—Marlon Brando may have top billing, but this is unquestionably a Johnny Depp film.

Brando took a shine to his young co-star during their first project together, and he gave freely of his life philosophy as well as offering Depp abundant professional advice. This included the suggestion that Depp consider reducing his workload, with the long haul in mind: "We only have so many faces," Brando noted. Much to Depp's surprise, the capricious elder statesman advised him to take on the challenging and often career-defining role of Hamlet before he was "too long in the tooth." While Depp has talked about subsequently making a point of reading

> *"It was tremendously exciting working with Marlon and Faye. They are actors with incredible careers. I was privileged to work alongside them and learn."*

Marlon Brando and Faye Dunaway as Dr. Jack Mickler and his wife Marilyn. Their stagnating marriage is revived by the arrival of the exotic Don Juan.

*Don Juan DeMarco* was apparently not the most enjoyable project for Depp, but the film received good reviews and made a respectable profit.

the play, there has never been any hint of his career taking a Shakespearean detour, though his newfound friendship with Brando continued, with the latter making an arresting cameo in Depp's ill-starred 1997 directorial debut *The Brave*.

It would appear that novice director Jeremy Leven may have been a little dazzled by the collective wattage of his two male stars, because Depp has talked about how he and Brando would sometimes rewrite unsatisfactory lines of dialogue just before the scene in question was to be filmed. Brando would then read the new material from discreetly positioned cue cards, which may explain some of the less impressive parts of his performance in *Don Juan DeMarco*.

In 1998, during a French television interview with Chiara Mastroianni (daughter of Marcello Mastroianni and Catherine Deneuve), Depp spoke frankly about the less than congenial mood on the set of a movie he'd made with a first-time director. Given the timing of the interview, the director in question could only be Jeremy Leven. "Sections of the dialogue were profound, beautiful, poetry, you know, and we went on the set with the guy

and—he believes that he's a master manipulator, but he's crap, you can see right through it," said Depp. "He was one of those guys who... refused to admit that he didn't know what he was doing. He wouldn't take advice from people, you see, he just forged ahead and it was really awful.

"I mean, we hit a point in that film where I actually had to tell the guy... you can say action, and cut, and print, if you like, but don't say anything else to me because I wanna kill you, you know, I'd really like to have my hands around your throat— so he didn't bother me any more, just stayed away. He said action, cut, print, wrap, and that was it."

The product of this strange and apparently fraught collaboration was released in April 1995, to be greeted with general approval in the entertainment press. More importantly for New Line Cinema, its gamble on Jeremy Leven paid off with a worldwide gross of nearly $70 million. Leven has not directed another studio film since, although he has developed a lucrative career as a writer of such mainstream fare as *The Legend of Bagger Vance* (2000), *Alex & Emma* (2003), and *The Notebook* (2004).

# Dead Man

1995

"Jarmusch is one of
my best friends and
also the movie director
I admire the most.
Why do anything just
for some money?"

Left: Thel Russell (Mili Avital) seduces Blake, a liaison that has fatal consequences for both of them.

Opposite: "I'm not dead. Am I?" Doomed accountant William Blake was Depp's first role in a Western, but with its brooding atmosphere and esoteric references this was no ordinary genre piece.

The opening sequence of Jim Jarmusch's black-and-white neo-Western *Dead Man* shows William Blake (Johnny Depp) leaving his native Cleveland on a west-bound train, having recently lost both of his parents. Blake—no relation to the visionary English poet of the same name—has spent his life savings on a ticket to a town named Machine, where he's been offered an accounting job. His optimism is somewhat dampened when the train's filthy yet mystical stoker (played by weirdo-for-hire Crispin Glover) invades Blake's personal space to give him a rambling, poetic speech and predict that Blake will die in Machine.

Blake's train journey virtually constitutes a film within a film; as the character ventures ever deeper into the American West, there is a marked and unsettling decline in the breeding and grooming of the passengers who board the locomotive; the Easterner—with his checked suit, floppy tie and fussy manner—looks increasingly incongruous as he glances skittishly at the untamed terrain all around him. After a full eight minutes of such longueurs, *Dead Man*'s titles finally start to roll. In 1996, a *Playboy* interviewer asked Depp how much he was paid for this film; rather than taking the usual tack of asking the writer if he'd ever discuss his own salary in public, Depp simply replied, "Less than my expenses during the shoot. But it's a poetic film. I did *Dead Man* so I could work with Jim Jarmusch. I trust Jim as a director, and a friend, and a genius."

Blake disembarks at Machine as a stranger in a strange land; and with Jarmusch at the helm things are bound to get even stranger. Depp's character arrives at his new place of employment, the toxic-looking Dickinson Metalworks, only to be informed by an insensitive functionary (played by John Hurt) that Machine has no need for another accountant. The beleaguered newcomer attempts to reason with factory owner John Dickinson—as portrayed by 78-year-old movie icon Robert Mitchum—who just stands beside a stuffed bear

and sneers down the barrel of his gun at the hapless bean-counter. (Any similarity between Dickinson and his ursine pal is presumably unintentional—although with Jarmusch, random whimsy and profound symbolism can easily become indistinguishable.)

Devastated, Blake staggers down Machine's muddy main drag, where he encounters Thel Russell (Mili Avital), a sometime prostitute who's making ends meet by selling paper flowers. Russell takes pity on Blake, and offers him horizontal comfort in her quarters. Their tryst is interrupted by Russell's boyfriend Charlie Dickinson (Gabriel Byrne), who shoots and kills the girl with a bullet that gravely wounds Blake after passing through her body. Depp's character somehow manages to kill his assailant with his third pistol shot. It transpires that the deceased cuckold is the spawn of bear-loving industrialist John Dickinson, who promptly dispatches a trio of mercenaries to hunt down his son's killer.

As he struggles to survive and evade capture in the inhospitable terrain surrounding Machine, Blake finds his savior in the form of a mystical Indian named Nobody (Gary Farmer), who—ostracized by two different Indian tribes as a result of his mixed parentage—is possibly even more of an outsider than Blake. Nobody (whose name appears to be an allusion to an episode in Homer's *Odyssey*) was apparently educated in England, and he can quote the words of visionary poet William Blake by the yard—it's unclear whether he believes Depp's character to be the reincarnation of his brilliant namesake, or whether he's just amused by the coincidence. Either way, Nobody prevents the "stupid white man" Blake from perishing in the wilderness, while admitting that he has no way to remove the potentially fatal bullet that remains lodged in Blake's chest.

The two unlikely companions continue to evade Blake's pursuers, and outwardly the accountant retains his sensible

*"It's a character that is, again, like a naïve young guy who's trying to get his life together. He's trying really hard to make his life work and he ends up slowly dying. And he knows he's dying. It's a beautiful story though."*

disposition; however, the depredations of life on the run have lent Blake's persona an increasingly flinty edge, and by murdering two US Marshals he proves that he is now a ruthless and efficient killer.

As Blake's health deteriorates, Nobody accelerates their hazardous journey to an old Indian encampment located beside a broad river. There, the barely conscious Blake is placed in a well-appointed, ocean-ready canoe, which is ceremonially launched seaward. In retrospect, this maritime denouement has a strange congruity with Depp's final words as Captain Jack Sparrow in the first *Pirates* movie: "Bring me that horizon!"

*Dead Man* maintains an unrelentingly brooding atmosphere throughout its two-hour time, and manages to acquire some unearned gravitas thanks to the composer of the film's score, Neil Young. Although sixties survivor Young has latterly become one of rock's critically untouchable figures, his *Dead Man* soundtrack is a ragged, well-intentioned experiment.

In deference to the musicians who would play along live with old-time movies, Young screened Jarmusch's film only once, spontaneously skipping between instruments to record whatever music came to his mind.

The *Village Voice*'s J. Hoberman boldly acclaimed *Dead Man* as a "visionary film," a bold assertion that was sadly drowned out by all the critics who uncharitably pointed out that Jarmusch's movie was borderline incomprehensible. One contributing factor is the director's promiscuous way with any allusion that takes his fancy.

Strangely enough, 15 years after making *Dead Man* Depp would find himself starring in a film that focused on very similar themes—the ravages of industrialization on the West, the smug venality of the new industrialist class—but which managed to hit its targets with gimlet-eyed accuracy and breathtaking velocity. The later film was *Rango*, the animated masterpiece in which Depp portrayed a skittish chameleon with a penchant for lucky breaks.

Opposite: Blake encounters a mystical Indian named Nobody (Gary Farmer), who helps him to survive for as long as possible before casting the mortally injured easterner out to sea in a canoe.

This page: While being pursued by bounty hunters, Blake takes time to grieve over a fawn and daubs his face with the animal's blood.

JOHNNY DEPP
S'il veut sauver
la vie de sa fille,
il a 90 minutes
pour devenir
un assassin.
MEURTRE EN SUSPENS

# Nick of Time

1995

.....................

"I've been accused of doing only strange films and oddball characters. I thought it was a good time to do the opposite— someone who is completely straight, a regular-Joe-type guy."

Over the years Johnny Depp has often been lauded for his decisions to turn down chances to appear in big-budget movies, even when those movies have gone on to be commercially successful. The most frequently cited blockbuster to which Depp gave the thumbs-down would probably be *Speed*, in which Keanu Reeves ended up taking the lead role. *Speed* had a conceit so breathtakingly stupid that one almost suspected that Hollywood had quietly replaced its traditional "give the public what they want" philosophy with the brutal new motto, "give the public what they deserve." The film, of course, made a fortune in every global market.

However, when Johnny Depp finally deigned to enter the action-movie arena it could hardly be claimed that his chosen vehicle—while superior to a cinematic insult like *Speed*—had any more merit than any of the multiplex mulch that Hollywood churned out on the average week. *Nick of Time* was a thriller with the simplest of premises: Depp's character Gene Watson arrives at Union Station, Los Angeles, with his young daughter; two villains snatch the daughter and hand Watson a gun, plus six bullets; if he wants to see his daughter again he has 90 minutes to assassinate California's governor. The plot owes more than a little to *The Man Who Knew Too Much* (both versions of which were directed by Alfred Hitchcock), and the decision to play out Watson's crucial 90 minutes in real time followed a format established in 1948 by Alfred Hitchcock's *Rope*, which was subsequently used by a handful of other directors (and ultimately flogged to death by the post-millennial television series *24*).

*Nick of Time* was directed by John Badham, who made the 1977 cultural phenomenon known as *Saturday Night Fever*, but who had long since settled into journeyman mode with pictures like *Stakeout* and *Bird on a Wire*. Depp expressed his admiration for Badham, spoke enthusiastically about getting the chance to work opposite that archest of arch-villains, Christopher Walken, and voiced his desire to play an ordinary citizen who is placed in an extraordinary situation. "I'm interested in story and character and doing things that haven't been done a zillion times," he told *Playboy*. "When I read *Nick of Time* I could see the guy mowing the grass, watering his lawn, putting out the Water Wiggle in the backyard for his kid, and I liked the challenge of playing him... it gives me a chance to play a straight, normal, suit-and-tie guy."

In Johnny Depp, Badham saw not just enormous untapped box-office potential, but an actor who perfectly fitted the archetype he needed for the Gene Watson part. "If Hitchcock were making this picture he'd have probably wanted Jimmy Stewart. Who's the Jimmy Stewart of the nineties?" he added rhetorically.

As Badham would soon discover, his star may have been able to revive the James Stewart archetype on screen, but his real life was something else entirely. The director spoke to *Premiere* magazine about his impression of Depp when he showed up for work at 7am every day. "I would think he was only propped up by a stage brace. He would stand there a little shaken, but totally focused."

Without laboring over the (few) strengths and (manifold) weaknesses of *Nick of Time*, or enumerating the logic flaws within the film's contrived plot, it is reasonably safe to say that Johnny Depp's first head-on dive into the mainstream turned out to be more of a belly flop. The film did not lack for publicity, particularly since Depp attended its Los Angeles premiere in November 1995 with tabloid-bait girlfriend Kate Moss on his arm; the public, however, just weren't buying it. *Nick of Time* failed to get much action at the US box office, with its receipts of just over $8 million representing a major loss for Paramount Pictures, the company that had paid Depp a reported $4.5 million to appear in its would-be blockbuster.

# Donnie Brasco

1997

...................

"When I did *Donnie Brasco*, people within the industry said, 'He finally played a man.' And I didn't particularly get it. It's like, why was I a man? Because I punched a couple of guys?"

*"It was a real treat and an honor... I expected him to be very serious and not very loose or playful, but he wasn't like that at all. He was constantly making jokes and making people laugh."*

Although there was no obvious case for making yet another Mafia picture toward the end of the last century, *Donnie Brasco* turned out to be a surprisingly diverting film that derived a substantial amount of its energy from Johnny Depp, who was at the time gaining recognition as an increasingly dependable character actor. *Newsweek* went so far as to state that Depp inhabited a higher artistic plane than more financially successful contemporaries like Brad Pitt and Keanu Reeves because, "he takes chances and he's created a body of work that actually makes sense when taken as a whole." The *Washington Post*, on the other hand, called Depp "a hunk with talent." Oh well, can't win 'em all.

Depp could hardly have asked for a better co-star on *Donnie Brasco* than Mob-movie veteran Al Pacino, who proves that he's still a formidable force even when he's playing the part of a morose, low-level Cosa Nostra soldier, and thus unable to display his trademark verbal pyrotechnics. The two men apparently got along very well during shooting of the film in early 1996, with Depp stating that his experience of working with Pacino was "everything and a whole lot more than I expected."

In the cinematic context of 1997 it seemed as though any new Mob film would be, by definition, obliged to operate within the familiar—possibly too familiar—territory that had been carved up between Messrs. Coppola and Scorsese over the previous two or three decades. The chances that anyone could find some new angle on the Sicilian business community seemed remote to say the least—but *Donnie Brasco* managed to offer its audience some fresh insight into the organized crime racket by focusing on the often mundane lives of operatives at the low end of the Mafia's food chain. In this respect, *Donnie Brasco* could legitimately claim to be a precursor to *The Sopranos*, a far more ambitious undertaking that helped introduce America's premium-cable viewers to the concept of expansive TV dramas (*The Wire* and *Game of Thrones* being

Left: *Donnie Brasco* tells the true story of FBI agent Joseph D. Pistone, who assumed a false identity in order to infiltrate two New York crime families.

Opposite: "Thirty years I'm busting my hump. What have I got?" As Donnie Brasco, Pistone wins the confidence of embittered hit man Benjamin "Lefty" Ruggiero (Al Pacino).

among the most lauded examples) whose creators tell their stories over the course of multiple seasons, letting them employ the kind of nuance and pacing that was once the exclusive domain of award-winning novels.

The fact that Johnny Depp could, in conjunction with Al Pacino, achieve so much within the context of a comparatively short, relatively low-key film is a tremendous credit to two actors whose fascinating one-off partnership is the driving force behind *Donnie Brasco*. The movie takes its name from the new identity allocated to real-life agent Joseph D. Pistone by his FBI paymasters in 1976, when he took on the deeply hazardous task of infiltrating New York's Bonanno and Colombo crime families. Pistone's assignment ended up lasting six years, wreaking havoc on his family life, and yielding more than 100 convictions—making it one of the most successful undercover operations in US history. In exchange for his admirable service to his country, Pistone was given $500 plus a medal at a closed-door ceremony.

Al Pacino plays Benjamin "Lefty" Ruggiero, a superannuated Mafia triggerman who knows that despite the 26 hits he has carried out on the organization's behalf, there is no guarantee that he'll be allowed to live long enough to enjoy a peaceful retirement. When Pacino's character isn't kvetching about his straitened circumstances, he's nervously glancing over his shoulder, forever expecting to become the victim of another Mafia hit. Ruggiero initially meets "Donnie Brasco" when the undercover cop is working under the guise of a Florida jewel thief—he wins Ruggiero's confidence by steering him away from fake merchandise, an act that leads Ruggiero unwittingly to take the undercover FBI agent under his wing as a protégé. After spending the best part of six years around the fatalistic Ruggiero and all his idiosyncrasies (apropos of nothing, the once-feared hit man will casually remark, "I've got cancer of the prick"), Depp's Pistone character can't help developing an affinity for the older man. Thanks to the absorbing, morally ambiguous relationship between its main two protagonists,

Donnie Brasco can be viewed as a buddy movie of sorts, albeit one of the most uneasy examples of the genre within recent memory.

In preparing to play the title role in Donnie Brasco, Depp spent significant time with Brooklyn wise guys, as did his director, the Englishman Mike Newell (best known for soft-serve comedies like Four Weddings and a Funeral). Newell was charmed by these real-life mafiosi, yet deeply disquieted by the brutality inherent in their vocational choice. Which might be why Donnie Brasco's director seems to be a little squeamish when it comes to depicting the quasi-operatic violence by which the Mafia instilled fear into millions of US citizens during much of the twentieth century. (Thanks to the diligence and bravery of law enforcement professionals like Joe Pistone, the Mob's power has now been severely curtailed.) Newell's personal sensitivities are a little hard on the moviegoing public, because he ends up eschewing the chance to tap into the reservoir of sociopathic rage that is Michael Madsen.

For long-time admirers of Johnny Depp, the comments made by Mike Newell after the release of Donnie Brasco—which, despite its generally favorable reviews, was only mildly successful in commercial terms—were every bit as fascinating as the film itself. Newell broke with movie-business omertà by offering up the kind of vivid description of Depp's true personality that strongly suggests that Depp has maintained a remarkable level of self-control during the many years he has spent under the scrutiny of the media. "He bit my ass a couple of times, and to this day I don't know what I did," Newell revealed. "There's a great deal more going on underneath than the sweet boy your mother would like. Somewhere along the line that sort of rackety life on the wrong side of the tracks has left a big mark, which, because he's so strong a character and so intelligent, he has disciplined; but once in a while, when he's not looking, something jumps out that is ancient and atavistic. But it's a mark of how decent a person he is that it's over almost instantaneously. You don't carry any resentment about it."

# The Brave

1997

.....................

"I never imagined how difficult it would be to act and direct at the same time."

*"Something in the story touched me deeply. The idea of sacrifice—how far will you go for those you love, for your family? It's a theme I'm fascinated by."*

For his directorial debut Depp chose the harrowing story of a Native American alcoholic who signs his life away for $50,000.

**B**y 1997 Johnny Depp had accrued sufficient *puissance* within his adopted industry to evolve into what the trade magazines call a "hyphenate"; in his case, an actor-writer-director. Depp decided that his first directorial gambit would be to adapt a harrowing novel called *The Brave*, written—implausibly enough—by Gregory Mcdonald, creator of the *Fletch* detective-book series (two of which were adapted into movie vehicles for comedian Chevy Chase). An early script of *The Brave* had first been shopped around Hollywood in 1993, to little avail; and even when Depp joined forces with the project's original producers the following year, potential investors continued to shy away from the project, which involves a young Native American man becoming embroiled in the lawless milieu of snuff movies.

Like the original novel, *The Brave* limns the tale of an alcohol-ravaged, barely-literate Native American character named Raphael (played by Depp), who lives in abject poverty near a city dump with his wife and two children. By the time Depp—who was now credited as a co-writer on the project—

had managed to find backers for *The Brave* (putting $2 million of his own money toward the film's reported budget of just under $10 million), it ended up being the Johnny Depp project that would have to follow the actor's most mainstream picture to date, the acclaimed Mob drama *Donnie Brasco*.

As *The Brave* gets underway, Raphael's life is hitting rock bottom; he happens to hear about a shady local businessman who is rumored to pay substantial sums to any individuals sufficiently desperate to accept the financial proposition at the cold heart of Mcdonald's book. The entrepreneur in question, known only as McCarthy, is played by Depp's *Don Juan DeMarco* co-star Marlon Brando, whom we first see sitting in a wheelchair in a capacious warehouse that contains only a torture chair.

The corpulent former icon explains to the hapless Raphael the precise nature of his proposition in a spellbinding soliloquy that recalls Colonel Kurtz, the character Brando portrayed so indelibly in Francis Ford Coppola's *Apocalypse Now*. Raphael is informed that his family will receive the sum of $50,000 if he allows himself to be tortured to death over the course of an hour in front of McCarthy's cameras. McCarthy goes on to give Raphael the details of this torture session in blood-curdling detail, and demands a response within 24 hours.

Unfortunately, *The Brave* starts to lose its way the instant Marlon Brando leaves the screen. The tone of Depp's film is wildly uneven, careening haphazardly between realism and fantasy, and periodically flirting with religious allegory and

nebulous portent in a desperate bid for higher significance. The director's attempts to illuminate the plight of Native Americans in modern-day America are undermined by *The Brave*'s inexplicable dearth of cultural specificity. There are several schools of thought about whether or not the central characters in movies must be sympathetic; but few would dispute the need for a leading man who is at least sensate, and on this particular occasion, Depp fails to clear even that hurdle as he drifts through the picture in a neurasthenic daze.

Hollywood insiders who passed judgment on initial screenings of the film deemed it to be "unwatchable," a theme on which reviewers were only too eager to expand. *Daily Variety*, for instance, dismissed *The Brave* as a "turgid and unbelievable

*"Marlon coming and doing this film for me was an incredible blessing. It was beyond a dream."*

neo-Western... strikingly preposterous," and *Screen International* said that the film "crawls across the screen for two hours like a snail." It seemed as though every critic in America was lining up to take a swing at Depp's cinematic piñata, and few of them missed their target. Only *Variety* managed to strike one positive note within an otherwise damning review, noting that—thanks to Slovenian cinematographer Vilko Filac—the movie was "handsomely mounted."

To his credit, Depp stood by his vision and endured the shit-storm of opprobrium with admirable equanimity. Not once did he resort to the default defense of the self-appointed "misunderstood artist" who assumes the fetal position and whines incessantly about how unfairly the world has judged him.

As if *The Brave* didn't already have enough serious problems, the film had been chosen as an Official Selection at the fiftieth Cannes Film Festival. Depp expressed his exasperation about being rushed into screening *The Brave* at such a high-profile event, but his protests were muted—possibly because the moviegoing public was unlikely to buy the idea that a global

box-office star who enjoyed his level of autonomy had not only made an irredeemable film, but also been coerced into showing it at one of the world's most prestigious festivals.

The most reasonable voice to be raised throughout this whole debacle was that of Depp's *Dead Man* co-star John Hurt, who bluntly declared that *The Brave* was unworthy of inclusion in the Cannes line-up, and criticized the festival's organizers for their desperation to showcase a major Hollywood celebrity at the event's fiftieth anniversary. Hurt made no personal attack on Depp, but instead expressed sympathy that the first-time director had let himself be flattered into exposing his inchoate product at such an inappropriate venue.

The fallout from all of this was that *The Brave* has never been released in the US, even in DVD form. For several years Depp's hardcore fans were obliged to hunt down ultra-rare bootleg copies of the film, but the inexorable rise of digital movie piracy means that it is now available to anyone with a decent Internet connection, whether they be super-fans or morbid curiosity-seekers.

"It was a crazy thing to do. That's not to say I regret it because I don't. But I would say it's not the most rational decision I've made in my life. I'm proud of it, but it was much more work than I anticipated."

"It's very nice to be appreciated, but I'm not really
comfortable with it. I've never liked being the center
of attention. It comes with the territory."

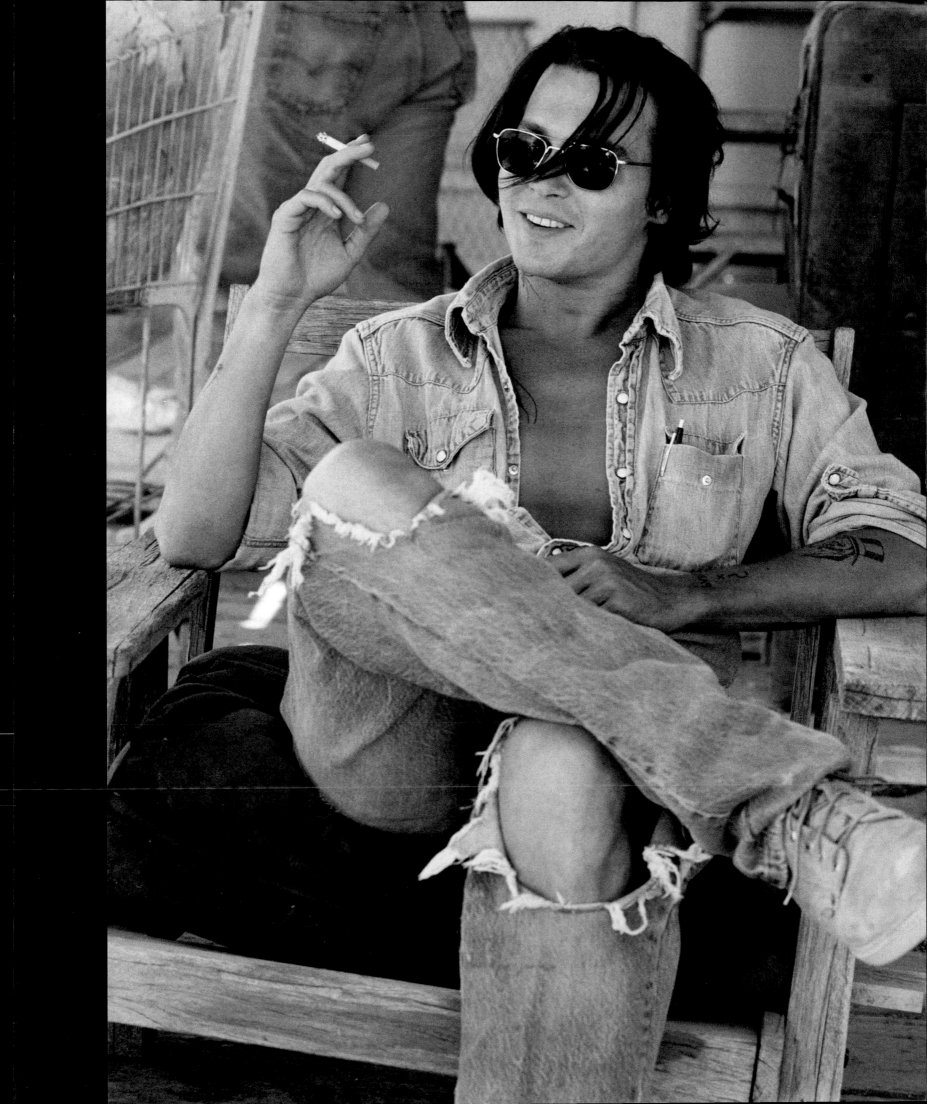

# Fear and Loathing in Las Vegas

1998

....................

"It was a whole
lot of fun, and a
whole lot of misery.
We got it all—the fear
and the loathing."

Johnny Depp first became a disciple of the writer Hunter S. Thompson during his teenage years, when older brother D.P. (Daniel) handed him a dog-eared copy of *Fear and Loathing in Las Vegas: A Savage Journey to the Heart of the American Dream*, which was possibly the apotheosis of Thompson's trademark "gonzo" journalism. (As the subtitle reveals, sardonic understatement was not part of the gonzo ethos.) Depp could never have guessed that he would one day star in a movie adaptation of the 1972 book, whose protracted journey to the big screen could almost be worthy of a book in its own right.

*Fear and Loathing* opened Johnny Depp's eyes to the young Thompson's super-charged lifestyle. It described a sojourn to Las Vegas—in the company of his corpulent lawyer, Oscar Acosta (referred to as "Dr. Gonzo" in the fictionalized account)—in order to write 250 words for *Sports Illustrated* on a motocross event. Upon their arrival in Vegas these two highly intoxicated gents found themselves face to face with all the garish horrors of America's new leisure frontier, equipped

only with a formidable cache of pharmaceuticals and a small arsenal of weaponry.

The novel—which originally appeared in November 1971 as a two-part *Rolling Stone* article in which Thompson gave his own character the name "Raoul Duke"—attained cult status during the culture wars of the Nixon era. As a hard-nosed junior reporter, Thompson was an ink-stained prodigy who'd scaled the journalistic ladder at an impressive rate; but his 1966 best-seller *Hell's Angels* represented a complete break with every tenet of traditional journalism, with the author placing himself at the very center of the action (and earning a severe beating by the eponymous motorcycle gang into the bargain).

With the 1968 election of Richard Nixon, Thompson donned his trademark pith helmet, bit down hard on his trademark cigarette holder, and proceeded to dazzle young America with his conservative-baiting tirades and Hogarthian tableaux; these stories, usually accompanied by the distinctively kinetic illustrations of Thompson's fellow-traveler Ralph Steadman,

*"I was freaked out by the idea of disappointing Hunter. So I did my best to absorb him. My goal was to steal his soul."*

*"Terry came in, grabbed it, shook it around and did it right. He's one of the best directors I've ever worked with, one of the most inventive, pure, organic experiences that I've had."*

"We were somewhere around Barstow, on the edge of the desert, when the drugs began to take hold." Director Terry Gilliam (above) was just the man to steer this freewheeling psychedelic road movie.

were by turns electrifying, dryly insightful, and blatantly untrustworthy. In order to distinguish himself from the other members of the emergent, non-objective New Journalism movement, Thompson—who'd become something of a talismanic figure at *Rolling Stone*—declared himself a "gonzo" journalist; this term became synonymous with various forms of inappropriate behavior and prodigious "derailment of the senses" within some of the most decorous temples of America's establishment.

Thompson viewed the grotesque excesses and moral hypocrisy of Straight America with a singularly absurdist attitude, which was enhanced by the steady ingestion of acid, peyote, ether, and a veritable doctor's bag of other illegal stimulants. If all else failed, there were always abundant reserves of hard liquor on hand; not to mention an impressive collection of ordnance, which Thompson regarded with a southern gentleman's sense of entitlement.

*Fear and Loathing*, with its convoluted, highly stylized internal monologues, seemed definitively unsuited to movie adaptation, but a couple of decades after its publication the freewheeling English director Alex Cox (*Repo Man*, *Sid and Nancy*) co-wrote a script with partner Tod Davies. During the early stages of the Cox project's production, two actors were repeatedly touted as candidates for the Thompson/Duke role: Leonardo DiCaprio and Johnny Depp. However, Cox fell out with the movie's producers, and also managed to offend Hunter Thompson in a fairly serious way. Thus it was that Minnesota-born director and *Monty Python* alumnus Terry Gilliam—himself no stranger to bare-knuckle fights with Hollywood

studios—was drafted in to rewrite the script within 10 days in May 1997, then film *Fear and Loathing* for under $19 million. The nettlesome issue of how to translate Thompson's original work into the reductive language of a motion picture had yet to be resolved, but Terry Gilliam was possibly the only major movie director who'd remain undaunted by that prospect.

Gilliam summed up the *Fear and Loathing* book with admirable frankness: "Although often nothing is really happening, everything is dramatized," he said. Even five years previously this would have been an insoluble problem, but Gilliam knew he could imbue the film with a new level of digital psychedelia thanks to recent developments in computer animation. Raoul Duke could therefore watch characters' faces morphing and melting before his eyes, while patterned casino carpets swirled like demonic lava beneath his unsteady feet.

One central factor in the film adaptation of *Fear and Loathing in Las Vegas* was the personal relationship between Hunter S. Thompson and Johnny Depp, the actor who was cast as Raoul Duke. Depp's reverence for the godfather of gonzo was still very much alive when the two men met socially in 1995; Depp made a pilgrimage to the Woody Creek Tavern, Thompson's fabled watering hole in Woody Creek, Colorado. It wasn't too long before the writer swaggered into the bar, and after a few rounds

*"No one has enough money to pay for the experience I've had on this movie. Going into the project, I knew that this would be our one time—and one time only—to make it right."*

Purple haze: The music and recreational habits of the counterculture feature prominently in the movie.

of drinks he found himself warming to the self-deprecating Hollywood pretty boy sitting opposite him.

After appropriate volumes of alcohol had been consumed, the new friends—who were born within 80 miles of each other in Kentucky, albeit 26 years apart—repaired to Thompson's isolated compound, where they proceeded to set off a homemade bomb and drink their way though the night.

In an effort to portray Thompson convincingly in *Fear and Loathing*, Depp prepared for his role by moving into the writer's basement for several weeks at a time, immersing himself in the writer's distinctive lifestyle. The normally recalcitrant Thompson accepted this unusual arrangement, even doing Depp the honor of shaving off his hair into an approximation of his own bald pate. During the course of his stay in Thompson's shabby basement, Depp rooted around for anything that might be useful to his imminent job, sometimes even alarming his host by wearing outfits that hadn't been washed since Thompson's *Fear and Loathing* period. The actor also dug up an unpublished early-sixties Thompson novel entitled *The Rum Diary*, based on the writer's experiences as a young reporter in Puerto Rico. Only a handful of people had ever been allowed to read the manuscript; Depp was so excited by the book that he insisted that, after the current film was wrapped, he and Thompson would sit down to discuss a movie adaptation.

When filming began on *Fear and Loathing*, these two transgenerational comrades found themselves separated by Terry Gilliam's canny decision to deny Hunter Thompson any access to the movie set. The writer nonetheless attempted to exert his influence upon the production by bombarding Depp and Gilliam with a series of hectoring faxes. The veteran Gilliam had no difficulty in ignoring this paper-storm, but Depp felt obliged to try to placate his friend.

It speaks volumes for Johnny Depp's professionalism that, even under this considerable pressure, he was still able to nail his scenes in just one or two takes. On the first day of shooting Depp was surprised to get a call from Bill Murray, who had

In *Fear and Loathing*, late 1990s CGI animation enabling swirling hotel carpets to come alive coexists with early 1970s word-processing technology.

A hallucinating Duke takes the phrase "lounge lizards" a little too literally.

taken a swing at playing Thompson in 1980, in the unsuccessful feature *Where the Buffalo Roam*. Murray wished Depp the best of luck, while cautioning him to "be careful when you play Hunter, because he never leaves. He'll never go away."

"Clearly I'd spent too much time with Hunter," Depp later admitted, "and it had taken over. There was something stronger than me on this film."

Johnny Depp brings a tremendous amount of heart to this movie, and he certainly cannot be faulted for his gravity-battling depiction of Thompson, his evocation of the writer's drug-induced paranoia, or the way he captures Thompson's habit of muttering dry asides in the manner of W.C. Fields. However, Terry Gilliam was not mistaken when he commented that "nothing is really happening" in *Fear and Loathing*; and there isn't an actor alive who could overcome an obstacle of that magnitude.

Gilliam's visual pyrotechnics are as iris-searingly inventive as anything ever seen on screen up to that point, but the onerous task of conjuring up a "story" from the available material predictably proved too much of a challenge. There are many purists who regard the use of a voice-over in any film as the last resort of the scoundrel; and in *Fear and Loathing* Terry Gilliam heavily employs just such a device in a vain attempt to evoke the ghost of gonzo past. (The voice in question does not belong to Depp, but to the less well known actor Donald Morrow.)

Benicio Del Toro put on a formidable amount of weight for the role of Raoul Duke's lawyer/accomplice, Dr. Gonzo,

Promoting the film at Cannes with co-star Benicio Del Toro and director Terry Gilliam. Depp's hair, which Hunter S. Thompson had shaved into an approximation of his own bald pate, has grown back and Del Toro is back down to his fighting weight.

and the actor lights up most of his scenes with an impressive range of apparently improvised comedic nonsense. Yet when all is said and done—and the peyote has finally worn off— we're basically left with an amiable and aimless road movie that may have worked better as a series of sketches on *Saturday Night Live*.

Predictably enough, *Fear and Loathing in Las Vegas* did not perform well at the US box office, and it sustained some harsh criticism from reviewers. Many of them viewed it as a countercultural relic that should have been left in its time capsule rather than hauled into modern-day multiplexes, where its anachronistic antics would never resonate with any viewer under 45. It was generally agreed that Depp had done himself great credit in the Raoul Duke role, although many critics were more fascinated by the often larger-than-life schtick of Del Toro, a relative newcomer to American movies.

Ten years after *Fear and Loathing*, Depp narrated a documentary on Thompson called *Gonzo* (and was jointly

nominated with Douglas Brinkley for a Grammy Award for the script-liner notes). The film began with a series of testimonials from friends who tacitly admitted that for much of his later life Hunter was barely able to muster up enough conviction to write. *Gonzo* was understandably elegiac in nature, having been made after Thompson had shot himself on February 20, 2005, at the age of 67.

Johnny Depp remained a True Believer to the end, following through on his stated intention to make a movie of *The Rum Diary*, which was released in 2011 with Depp in a role closely based on the young Hunter S. Thompson. At a memorial service six months after Thompson's death, Depp had come good on another promise: to dispose of the writer's ashes according to his highly specific instructions. This involved firing the ashes, in several containers, from a custom-made cannon that reportedly cost Depp $2 million. The weapon was mounted on a 153-foot tower featuring a large-scale rendering of Thompson's famous logo: a fist with two thumbs, clutching a peyote button.

# The Ninth Gate

1999

"It's classic Polanski.
If you took *Rosemary's
Baby* and *Chinatown* and
mixed them together,
it would be this movie."

*"It was not an easy film to make. Roman is pretty set in his ways. There's not much opportunity for discussion or collaboration. He was definitely a bit too rigid for my liking."*

Left: Johnny Depp and Roman Polanski deep in thought, but not conversation.

Opposite bottom: City-hopping with his mysterious guardian angel as played by Polanski's wife, Emmanuelle Seigner.

When Johnny Depp signed up to star in the Paris-based supernatural thriller *The Ninth Gate*, his principal motivation was the chance to work with the venerable Polish-born director Roman Polanski (who fled to the French capital from the United States in 1978 on the eve of being sentenced for having unlawful sex with a minor). According to Depp, the film's script was, "sort of like, all right, you know. Maybe when we can get in there, we can float around a little bit and find some stuff and change it."

Depp and Polanski's working relationship on the movie—which was adapted from *The Club Dumas*, a 1993 novel by the Spanish writer Arturo Pérez-Reverte—did not exactly begin in a blaze of collaborative passion. Not only was Polanski, as one of the movie's co-writers, opposed to Depp's "floating around" idea; he was initially uncertain about Depp's suitability to replace John Travolta in the role of opportunistic rare-book dealer Dean Corso. Travolta left the project in high dudgeon

after certain changes were made to the script, and there was talk of litigation to follow. However, once shooting was underway Polanski was reassured by Depp's openness, spontaneity, and keen intelligence.

The film begins with Depp's goateed and bespectacled Corso character being approached by a wealthy, suave, and slightly depraved-looking book collector named Boris Balkan (Frank Langella), who offers to remunerate him handsomely should he accomplish the tricky task of hunting down and authenticating the two other remaining copies of a specific book he owns: *The Nine Gates of the Kingdom of Shadows* (published 1666). In the course of his initial inquiries, Corso discovers that some of the individuals believed to possess copies of *The Nine Gates* have been meeting with various unpleasant fates. He also hears some bizarre rumors suggesting that whoever manages to gather together the three original copies of *The Nine Gates* will gain access to a doorway that leads to... *another world?*

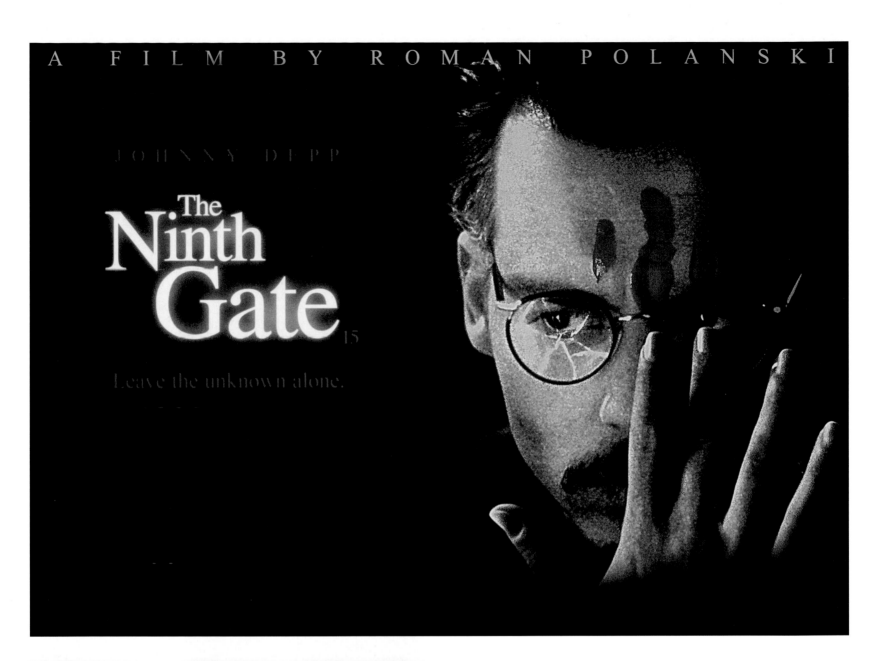

JOHNNY DEPP

The Ninth Gate 15

Leave the unknown alone.

Corso's quest to locate the tomes and initiate a display of Mr. Balkan's largesse takes him to various European cities. At a certain point he realizes that he is being tracked by shadowy individuals intent on bringing his assignment to a premature and possibly violent end; Corso—whom Depp imbues with a mordant humor and suspicious mien—is repeatedly rescued by a seemingly omnipresent and quite possibly supernatural sprite who is identified only as "The Girl" (and played by Polanski's wife, Emmanuelle Seigner).

Corso's city-hopping biblio-quest becomes so convoluted that the viewer quickly starts to feel more exhausted than he does. The film's Byzantine plot takes so many implausible detours that one can almost envision Roman Polanski hunched over a laptop on the movie's set, frantically cranking out fresh pages in the desperate hope of getting the film's plot finally to make sense.

The climactic phase of *The Ninth Gate* occurs at a remote, heavily guarded mansion that appears to be hosting some

kind of *Eyes Wide Shut* theme party for well-heeled Satanists. While viewers are still reeling at the bare-faced audacity of Polanski's "homage" to Stanley Kubrick, Frank Langella's Boris Balkan character bursts into the mansion's ballroom, pre-empting preparations for a black mass with his manic cries of "Mumbo jumbo!"

The release of *The Ninth Gate* engendered something of a debate regarding Polanski's intentions in making such an outlandish picture: On the one hand there were those who smiled and nodded along knowingly as they watched the film, savoring its supposedly playful tone; the opposing camp took the movie as conclusive proof that the director had lost his touch, if not more. Kenneth Turan of the *Los Angeles Times* was somewhere between the two camps, remarking

that he found *The Ninth Gate*'s steady flow of genre clichés to be quite comforting.

Although *The Ninth Gate* failed to burnish Johnny Depp's reputation, the circumstances of the movie's creation ended up having a profound impact upon his life. While filming in

Opposite: In this darkly comic and fiendishly complex supernatural thriller, Depp plays Dean Corso, a rare-book dealer hired to track down the two remaining copies of a seventeenth-century satanic text.

Right: Depp and Polanski celebrate the completion of *The Ninth Gate* in a Paris bar, April 1998.

France, Depp chanced upon one of the country's minor cultural treasures, the actress/singer Vanessa Paradis. At the age of 14, Paradis had a hit with a lounge-jazz novelty song entitled "Joe le taxi," and she went on to make the occasional popular album, one of which—a self-titled work from 1992—was produced by her then-boyfriend, the American retro-rocker Lenny Kravitz. Paradis's acting career had an auspicious beginning: For her 1989 cinematic debut, *Noce Blanche*, she won a César (the Gallic equivalent of an Oscar) for Most Promising Actress.

While Paradis traded in some of her abundant cultural equity for well-paid advertising gigs—including a highly lucrative stint in TV and print ads for Chanel fragrances—this lady was clearly more accomplished than the model girlfriend with whom Johnny Depp had split up a couple of years earlier. Paradis and Depp had met briefly several years before *The Ninth Gate*, but when they became reacquainted in Paris in the lobby of the Hôtel Costes (a long-time fashion-world favorite),

Depp and Paradis began dating, and shortly thereafter she became pregnant *pour la première fois*.

Depp soon elected to make France his new home, mainly because he considered the country an ideal place in which to raise a family; and, to a lesser extent, because of the nation's laissez-faire attitude toward smoking. Since Depp had already made onerous work commitments before meeting his new inamorata, it was decided that Paradis would spend the majority of her pre-natal months ensconced in her family's home.

In late 1998 Depp made a quick jaunt across the English Channel to London, to meet his old comrade Tim Burton, who was in the midst of pre-production for his cinematic take on one of America's most enduring literary yarns. "The Legend of Sleepy Hollow" is a supernatural tale written by Washington Irving in 1819, and Burton's version was to feature Johnny Depp. The resulting movie would prove almost as serendipitous as Depp's random Paris encounter with Mlle Paradis.

# The Astronaut's Wife

1999

...................

"It was fun to play a redneck, an all-American hero gone wrong... I definitely didn't like him, that's for sure."

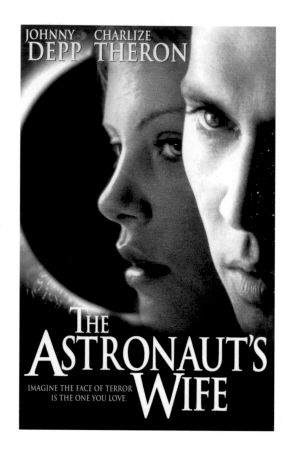

Something's not right:
Commander Spencer
Armacost (Depp) receives a
hero's welcome on his return
from space, but he's not the
man he used to be.

After *Don Juan DeMarco*, Johnny Depp vowed never again to work with a first-time director. Which makes his decision to sign up for the putative thriller *The Astronaut's Wife*, written and directed by debutant Rand Ravich, rather baffling. Doubly so if you consider the content of Ravich's original script: The basic premise of the story might have made for a perfectly adequate episode of a TV series like Rod Serling's *Twilight Zone*, but in the context of contemporary cinema this was the kind of material that could only ever aspire to being a solid B-movie. Although Hollywood did not consider Depp to be a certified A-list actor at this point, he still maintained the kind of bankability that gave him the ability to choose between taking well-paid, high-profile jobs and working with some of the most accomplished and distinctive directors in the business. Yet once again, with *The Astronaut's Wife* Depp opted for a project that did not fall into either of those categories.

Depp plays Commander Spencer Armacost, whose most recent assignment was a near-disastrous space-shuttle mission that involved an alarming two-minute loss of contact with the NASA control room during a spacewalk with his colleague Alex Streck (Nick Cassavetes). As Armacost settles back into terrestrial domesticity with his young wife, Jill (Charlize Theron), Ravich begins to let us know just how significant that disturbing 120-second interlude may have been. After the seemingly stoic Alex Streck loses his mind and dies, Streck's wife commits suicide; then Armacost's wife discovers that she's pregnant, and becomes seriously unsettled as she watches her once-feisty husband losing his personality and transforming into a manically overprotective father-to-be. This appears to be the aspect of the Armacost role that persuaded Depp to overcome his allergy to neophyte directors. "With all of us I think there is more to it than meets the eye," he told the *Calgary Herald* in late 1999. "I like the idea that on the surface this guy

Having flirted with disaster, Armacost reacquaints himself with his wife Jill (Charlize Theron).

> *"It was a pretty suspenseful script...*
> *I thought it was a very well-written story.*
> *A really interesting idea."*

was a charming, healthy all-American guy, but at the very seed of his being he is a sort of a vicious animal."

All too soon it becomes apparent that Johnny Depp's character must be possessed—possessed by the spirit of every demon-seed movie ever made, from *Village of the Damned* to *Rosemary's Baby* to *Alien*. Unfortunately, the most frightening thing about *The Astronaut's Wife* is the familiarity and profusion of its influences; modern moviegoers are so accustomed to genres being deconstructed, turned inside out and generally played with that many of them probably suspected that this film could easily turn into a full-blown *Airplane!*-style parody at any moment—but just like the thrills, the laughs never come.

In Depp and Theron *The Astronaut's Wife* could hardly have had two co-stars who combined to make a more handsome couple, and it can hardly be said that there's a complete lack of chemistry between these two, who have some convincingly frisky scenes together before things take a turn for the supernatural. (When Depp's character is briefly allowed to talk to his wife during the fateful space mission, his first question is, "What are you wearing?") But the derivative nature of the plot only reminds us that two years previously Theron acted in *The Devil's Advocate*, a far more convincing variation on the same theme. Meanwhile, we finally get to see Johnny Depp undertaking the challenge that has long been mandatory for any actor with major-league aspirations: the Southern Accent. Depp may have been raised in mainland America's southernmost state, but the deracinated dialect he employs in this picture serves as a reminder that only a small part of northern Florida has a true sense of southern

*"It was the opportunity to play one of these guys who has the pearly white smile... when in fact he's just a monster."*

ethnicity. For Depp, this questionable accent is a rare misstep that might suggest that he's mortal after all.

Veteran cinematographer Allen Daviau (an occasional Steven Spielberg collaborator) gives *The Astronaut's Wife* a silvery patina of Good Taste that only serves to highlight the numerous fatal flaws within the story. Still, this would be a tolerable enough piece of generic entertainment were one to stumble across it late at night on a basic-package cable channel—however, once again it's hard to imagine what moved Johnny Depp to sign up for a picture so clearly incommensurate with his own professional standing.

*The Astronaut's Wife* was produced by New Line Cinema, a company that didn't exactly give the film a vote of confidence when it decided not to arrange advance screenings for US critics. It was a strategy that led many to suspect that this particular astronaut must be a dog, something that was confirmed when the reviews finally appeared; in commercial terms the film

imploded on the launch-pad—once again we were shown that Johnny Depp was not yet a big enough name to "open" a movie. *The Astronaut's Wife* earned only around $12 million at the domestic box office, which meant that New Line was still light years away from recouping the film's $34 million budget (plus attendant marketing costs).

Depp is unlikely to have lost sleep over this picture's less-than-stellar financial performance, since his personal repute always seemed to emerge unscathed from whatever throwaway project he happened to stroll through in any given year. For instance, while the *New York Times* condemned *The Astronaut's Wife* to a definitively lukewarm review, the paper's critic Manohla Dargis charitably noted that, "Depp moves through the film suavely and imperturbably, never letting the particulars bog him down." The apparently bullet-proof aura that surrounded Johnny Depp became ever more intriguing as his career "arc" began to look more and more like the design for a theme-park ride.

*People say I make strange choices, but they're not strange for me. My sickness is that I'm fascinated by human behavior, by what's underneath the surface, by the worlds inside people."*

# Sleepy Hollow

1999

.................

"I thought of Ichabod as a very delicate, fragile person who was maybe a little too in touch with his feminine side, like a frightened little girl."

# HEADS WILL ROLL

A TIM BURTON FILM

*Sleepy Hollow*

## JOHNNY DEPP · CHRISTINA RICCI

PARAMOUNT PICTURES AND MANDALAY PICTURES PRESENT A SCOTT RUDIN/AMERICAN ZOETROPE PRODUCTION A TIM BURTON FILM
JOHNNY DEPP CHRISTINA RICCI "SLEEPY HOLLOW" MIRANDA RICHARDSON MICHAEL GAMBON CASPER VAN DIEN JEFFREY JONES
MUSIC BY DANNY ELFMAN COSTUME DESIGNER COLLEEN ATWOOD PRODUCTION DESIGNER RICK HEINRICHS EDITED BY CHRIS LEBENZON DIRECTOR OF PHOTOGRAPHY EMMANUEL LUBEZKI CO-PRODUCER KEVIN YAGHER
EXECUTIVE PRODUCERS FRANCIS FORD COPPOLA LARRY FRANCO BASED UPON THE STORY BY WASHINGTON IRVING SCREEN STORY BY KEVIN YAGHER AND ANDREW KEVIN WALKER
 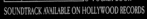 READ THE POCKET BOOK SCREENPLAY BY ANDREW KEVIN WALKER PRODUCED BY SCOTT RUDIN ADAM SCHROEDER DIRECTED BY TIM BURTON
SOUNDTRACK AVAILABLE ON HOLLYWOOD RECORDS NOVEMBER

www.sleepyhollowmovie.com

"In a way it's a homage to all those Dracula and Hammer House of Horror films of the 1960s, with a style of acting that's just on the verge of being acceptable. Maybe it's a little over the top."

Having experienced mixed fortunes since their last collaboration five years previously, Johnny Depp and Tim Burton resumed their telepathic working relationship on *Sleepy Hollow*.

At the point when Johnny Depp reunited with director Tim Burton to make *Sleepy Hollow*—five years after they'd worked together on *Ed Wood*—there had been a marked divergence in their respective careers. Depp made a disastrous directorial debut with *The Brave*, a film that was shown prematurely at the 1997 Cannes Film Festival due to the organizers' desperate need to snag a celebrity name for the event's fiftieth anniversary. However, he managed to bounce back relatively quickly with the Terry Gilliam adaptation of *Fear and Loathing in Las Vegas*, the 1970s cult novel by Hunter S. Thompson. While this project was by no means a commercial triumph, it certainly went some way toward rehabilitating Johnny Depp's damaged reputation. The movie's reviews tended to come down on the positive side of "mixed," but there was nary a discouraging word about his portrayal of Thompson's alter ego, Raoul Duke.

On a personal level Depp had gone through a four-year relationship with the English model Kate Moss before meeting the future mother of his children, the French star Vanessa Paradis, while he was in Paris working on the Roman Polanski thriller *The Ninth Gate*.

Tim Burton, meanwhile, had endured his first box-office failure in 1996 with *Mars Attacks!*, a picture that broke the improbably long run of successive hits that reached all the way back to his 1985 debut, *Pee-wee's Big Adventure*. An unfortunate stumble, to be sure, but nothing serious enough to deter Warner Bros. from offering Burton $5 million to direct its planned revival of the Superman franchise. Few could fault Burton for taking a gun-for-hire gig at this point in his career, particularly since the Warner deal stipulated that he'd be paid in full whether or not the movie ever went into production. However, as Burton would find out, a Hollywood contract that guaranteed payment did not also promise a happy working relationship.

When Burton took over the reins of Warner's Superman project, the studio had already hired and fired—at great expense—two writers. A third writer, the indie auteur and comic-books obsessive Kevin Smith, had recently come in and written a brand-new version of the script, entitled *Superman Lives*. Burton—who had turned another of the company's superhero properties into a globe-straddling phenomenon with his 1989 blockbuster *Batman*—felt that he needed to start the whole process from scratch, so he promptly brought in a fourth writer of his own choosing. Warner Bros. had signed up a leading man, Nicolas Cage, who was guaranteed to receive the best part of $20 million whether or not the cameras ever rolled, but with every passing month Burton became less convinced that the company actually knew what it wanted. He felt the Superman movie was being "committee-ized to death," and like many directors before him resented all the random, unsolicited input he was getting from Warner Bros. head of production Jon Peters.

"I basically wasted a year," Burton said when Warner Bros. finally decided to put Superman's cape back in mothballs after throwing away around $30 million. "A year is a long time to be working with somebody you don't really want to be working with." After a couple of halfhearted attempts to start work on new movie projects, Burton appeared to transform his frustration into creative energy. And in doing so he ended up creating a film that remains to this day the apotheosis of his ongoing professional relationship with Johnny Depp.

*Sleepy Hollow* started out as a story written by Washington Irving and published in the US and UK during 1819 and 1820 in his pseudonymous, self-published collection *The Sketch Book of Geoffrey Crayon, Gent.*, which also showcased "Rip Van Winkle."

The protagonist of the original "The Legend of Sleepy Hollow"—inspired by a German folktale and written in a breezy style some critics described as "sportive Gothic"—was a gawky, odd-looking teacher named Ichabod Crane, who had a late-night encounter with a Headless Horseman near Tarrytown, New York. "Sleepy Hollow" took immediate root in the American psyche, and over subsequent decades has been reiterated numerous times in the cinema and on stage (including several musical versions).

Even without the use of prosthetics, Depp managed to capture the gawkiness of Ichabod Crane, while still satisfying the studio's desire for his leading-man looks, as displayed next to co-star Christina Ricci (opposite).

*"Playing Ichabod was a great challenge. This is a character we grew up knowing very well, and of course I incorporated all the stuff from the book. But Paramount wouldn't let me wear a long nose and big ears."*

Any public awareness of "Sleepy Hollow" that existed before Tim Burton's big-budget 1999 movie can likely be traced back to the 1949 Disney cartoon *The Adventures of Ichabod and Mr. Toad*, which for financial reasons conjoined Washington Irving's creation with Kenneth Grahame's *The Wind in the Willows*. Forty-five years on, Kevin Yagher—a makeup effects designer who'd directed two episodes of the HBO series *Tales from the Crypt*—got the urge to write a screenplay based on the original "Sleepy Hollow," adding to Irving's short story enough new ideas to justify a full-length feature.

Yagher collaborated on the project with Andrew Kevin Walker, who was about to gain notoriety as the writer of the grisly 1995 suspense thriller *Se7en*. Yagher and Walker produced a 20-page *Sleepy Hollow* treatment that was optioned in 1994 by high-profile producer Scott Rudin, who subsequently sold the idea to Paramount Pictures. There was no further movement on the *Sleepy Hollow* front until 1998, when Rudin sent a copy of the script to Tim Burton, whose dance card was empty for the first time in a decade. Burton liked what he read, and agreed to

take on the project. The director wanted Johnny Depp to play Ichabod Crane, but—even at this stage in Depp's career—he first had to persuade Paramount executives to sign off on the idea.

At Scott Rudin's suggestion *Sleepy Hollow* was shot (between November 1998 and April 1999) in England. Burton intended to find some suitably archaic hamlet to use as the film's backdrop, but for various reasons this proved impractical, so *Sleepy Hollow* ended up being made on two soundstages big enough to accommodate elaborate recreations of nineteenth-century Hudson Valley tableaux. Production designer Rick Heinrichs explained the prevailing aesthetic as "a kind of natural expressionism," and in terms of special effects, Burton—who filled his sets with "atmospheric" smoke— preferred old-school authenticity over the digital trickery of CGI, a proclivity that entailed a good deal of improvisation from the film's technical crew.

Burton had no intention of making this film in black and white, and he brought in Mexican cinematographer Emmanuel Lubezki, who is renowned for the way he uses color filters to

give films a highly distinctive color palette; thanks to Lubezki *Sleepy Hollow* glows with an otherworldly luminescence, its tone hovering somewhere in the middle of the spectrum between monochrome and color. Burton aimed to "capture the beautiful, lurid atmosphere of the old Hammer films," and to this end, the director asked his old comrade Johnny Depp to give him a style of performance that would fit into one of the many popular horror movies produced by England's Hammer Films during its mid-century heyday. Depp later told an interviewer how he interpreted Burton's request. "It's acting in a style that wouldn't normally be acceptable in a regular movie," Depp explained. "If it's a little bad, it's good, you know."

(When it came time for *Sleepy Hollow*'s main players to hit the promotional trail on the movie's behalf, the name of Hammer Films was never far from their lips. It almost seemed as though they'd been programmed to reference Hammer at every possible opportunity—even though the final product bears virtually no resemblance to any of Hammer's highly distinctive productions.)

Depp had assumed that he'd be using prosthetic makeup to reincarnate Irving's original Ichabod Crane, with his cartoonish "feet that could have served as shovels," and the general mien of an escaped scarecrow. The actor was therefore surprised to find out that no such transformation was in Tim Burton's plans; so Depp reached into his thespian's bag of tricks to look for some real-life person whose distinctive mannerisms could be grafted onto his version of the Ichabod character. Depp made the counterintuitive decision to focus on the English actress Angela Lansbury, paying particular attention to her earliest films; after adding just a hint of Roddy McDowall's fastidiousness, Depp gives us an Ichabod who possesses not one of the characteristics we identify with a leading-man role.

Burton did not so much cast *Sleepy Hollow* as curate it. With great acuity he cherry-picked the actors who would surround Johnny Depp in the film, including peerless British character actors like Michael Gambon, Miranda Richardson, and Richard Griffiths. For the role of Ichabod Crane's budding love interest Katrina Van Tassel, the director selected former

Opposite: Shooting in England with renowned cinematographer Emmanuel Lubezki helped Burton to "capture the beautiful, lurid atmosphere" of the horror films produced by British studio Hammer in the 1950s and 1960s.

Right: "Then have a kiss on account." In an embrace with Christina Ricci, whom Tim Burton imagined as the love child of Peter Lorre and Bette Davis.

child hipster Christina Ricci, who was once memorably described by *Cahiers du Cinéma* as "the up-and-coming 'muse' of American goth culture." Tim Burton's description of the actress was somewhat more specific: "If Peter Lorre and Bette Davis had a child, it would be Christina."

There was a non-speaking part as the Headless Horseman for Christopher Walken, with a couple of scenes that only used—courtesy of blue-screen filming—the actor's severed head, replete with filed-down teeth. Although the New York-born Walken is far from a natural equestrian, he did enough training to make his horseback scenes look convincing. Johnny Depp, on the other hand, ended up using a mechanical horse for some of his riding obligations—the very same piece of equipment that the young Elizabeth Taylor used in her 1944 equestrian melodrama *National Velvet*.

In Kevin Yagher and Andrew Kevin Walker's reworking of the old "Sleepy Hollow" fable, Ichabod Crane is a New York detective whose dogmatic belief that all crimes can be solved by scientific means gets him banished from the city. He is given an assignment that takes him up the Hudson Valley to the town of Sleepy Hollow, where three recent murders will provide him with ample opportunity to prove the validity of his forensic theories. Since all three victims were beheaded, the population of Sleepy Hollow believes that the killer comes from a dark realm that you can't read about in any scientific textbook. Twenty years earlier, a Hessian (German) mercenary was killed in a battle at Sleepy Hollow, then buried in an unmarked grave: The locals believe that this is the folk-devil responsible for the atrocities that have just occurred in their community, within the space of one week.

During *Sleepy Hollow*'s pre-production stage, Tim Burton had the nagging feeling that the current draft of the movie's script felt a little unleavened, so he hired venerable English playwright/screenwriter Tom Stoppard to punch it up with a few gags, and add some high-tone filigree to the dialogue. While working on this well-paid but uncredited rewrite Stoppard decided that the existing plot structure would also be improved if he could create more connections between the film's characters; but his

which are just non-functional visual treats for the film's viewers) might as well be the tools of the devil himself. However, as the body count continues to grow, the locals come to accept Crane as the one man who might just be able to stop the slaughter.

During his stay in Sleepy Hollow, Ichabod is a houseguest of the wealthy Van Tassel family, and despite his apparently feminine frailty he begins to fall under the spell of the daughter Katrina (Christina Ricci). The question is, exactly what kind of spell is it, because at one point he awakes to find Katrina drawing various occult symbols on the floor around his bed. But, as we eventually discover, there is only one true witch under this roof, and that's Katrina's stepmother, Lady Van Tassel, played by Miranda Richardson at her elegantly malevolent best.

It is worth noting that Johnny Depp's *Sleepy Hollow* performance is among his very best—all the talk about Angela Lansbury is amusing, but no one should forget that the creation of characters as extraordinary as Ed Wood and

laborious efforts to do so only had the effect of complicating the narrative to the point where—when the dust finally settles and the blood stops flowing—the internal logic of *Sleepy Hollow* cannot really withstand close scrutiny. (Then again, as many of Tim Burton's admirers will admit, crafting watertight plots has never really been among his major concerns.)

The initial phase of the story establishes Ichabod Crane as the proverbial fish out of water, a New York City detective who arrives in the boondocks to try to work among the insular, superstitious natives who greet him there. The townsfolk of Sleepy Hollow are extremely suspicious of Ichabod's forensic approach to crime-solving, which they regard as tantamount to heresy; and his array of new-fangled instruments (most of

Ichabod and Katrina recoil in horror as the Headless Horseman is unleashed from the murky depths below the Tree of the Dead. The goriness of *Sleepy Hollow* ensured that it received an "R" rating.

Ichabod Crane cannot be done by using a few cute tricks. For all his witty self-deprecation, Depp is clearly someone who possesses a great level of craftsmanship, and who always wants to find new ways to expand his range. It shouldn't be surprising that, surrounded by talents of this magnitude, Christina Ricci gives what is probably the least mannered and most effective performance of her career.

Frustrated at his own lack of progress toward apprehending the pre-modern serial killer, Crane agrees to let Katrina take him to a local witch who can lead them to the Tree of the Dead, where the Hessian rider is buried. They find his head (played by Christopher Walken) among the tree's mangled roots, then recoil in terror as the Headless Horseman himself bursts forth from the mephitic depths below.

The first autopsy Ichabod Crane performs in the course of his investigation involves the Headless Horseman's fifth victim, a pregnant woman. Burton ratchets up the fear factor by revealing that in addition to beheading this woman the Headless Horseman has done the same thing to her fetus.

If they were going to give this Tim Burton film an "R" rating he was going to make sure he made the most of it.

The bloodthirsty Sturm und Drang that is unleashed by the Headless Horseman during the final furlong of *Sleepy Hollow* sets the audience's heads spinning so fast that it doesn't have a chance to worry about the various plot holes and loose ends that have been strewn across Burton's spooky landscape. As one would expect, there were plenty of critics keeping a tally of the flaws in *Sleepy Hollow*'s script, although most reviewers appreciated the film as a great sensory pleasure, and only made passing mention of its shortcomings.

With domestic receipts of around $100 million, and the same again in the rest of the world, *Sleepy Hollow* served to remind Hollywood that however weird Tim Burton might look, his name was virtually synonymous with profit. There was also the bonus of three Oscar nominations, one of which yielded an Academy Award for Best Art Direction (Set Decoration). This is a film that represents a phenomenon almost as rare as the Headless Horseman: the harmonious marriage of art and commerce.

# The Man Who Cried

2000

....................

"Each film... that
I make, more than
it is a career move
or anything like that,
it's just an extended
education each time."

*"To me the gypsies—I feel uncomfortable saying the word since they are all people—but they paralleled the Native Americans in this country and what happened ever since Whitey stepped foot on American soil here. It's been that way for the gypsies, so The Man Who Cried was a great opportunity to get to know those people and where they come from."*

The first part of Johnny Depp's millennial gypsy duology (the second being *Chocolat*), *The Man Who Cried* required little heavy lifting from the actor. Depp had fewer than a dozen lines in the entire picture, in which he played a gypsy horse-trainer named Cesar—even more than his role as Roux in *Chocolat*, this one required him to maintain a convincingly sultry presence whenever he appeared, which he managed to do without any visible effort. At the beginning of the millennium, Depp was at a point in his career where every other project seemed to involve a reunion with someone from an earlier film—in this case it was Christina Ricci, the young actress who worked with him on *Sleepy Hollow* and *Fear and Loathing in Las Vegas*. Depp first encountered Ricci as far back as 1990, on the set of the romantic comedy *Mermaids*,

when she was a nine year old making her acting debut as the little sister of Depp's then-girlfriend Winona Ryder. It was perhaps just a little bizarre, 10 years later, to see him taking on a supporting role in a film that features Ricci in its lead role; not to mention the fact that Depp—who was born some 17 years before his round-faced co-star—was involved in her first cinematic love scene. "It's weird to think of having sex with him," said Ricci. "But we know enough about each other to laugh at it."

There isn't a great deal to laugh about in *The Man Who Cried*, an art-house film with epic aspirations; directed by Sally Potter (best known for the quasi-mystical, gender-bending period piece *Orlando*), the movie spans several decades and half the circumference of the globe. The story begins with the parents

of Ricci's character, Fegele, getting caught up in Russia's anti-Jewish pogroms of the 1920s, and sending their little girl to safety in England. There she must live with cruel foster parents, who give her the name Suzie and forbid her to speak Yiddish.

Thanks to Suzie's burgeoning talent as a singer, she's able to find work at a Paris cabaret, where she is taken under the wing of a glamorous, flint-hearted Russian showgirl named Lola. The latter is played by Cate Blanchett, who endows her character with a thick layer of blood-red lipstick and a gold digger's wicked sense of camp. Lola's opera-singer boyfriend Dante Dominio, as depicted by John Turturro, may not wear lipstick, but Turturro does not lose out to Blanchett in the scenery-chewing stakes, imbuing his pompous, Mussolini-loving Italian with an ego the size of La Scala. In comparison

to such outrageous vulgarians, Johnny Depp's humble horse-trainer Cesar cannot help but look mild-mannered, but—much to Lola's horror—Ricci cannot resist his smoldering good looks, or the earthy outsider culture to which he belongs.

*The Man Who Cried* further stretches the accepted parameters of the art-house movie by embracing a level of melodrama that might border on the preposterous in less illustrious company. As World War II engulfs Europe, and the Nazis begin to encroach upon Paris, Suzie is forced to leave the continent; she makes the interminable schlep to Los Angeles, in search of her long-lost father. Suffice it to say that the denouement of Potter's picture replaces the elegant backdrop of L'Opéra with the less salubrious tone of Hollywood soap opera, creating a potential risk for diabetic viewers.

# Before Night Falls

2000

..................

"Julian Schnabel called and asked if I wanted to play a small part as a transvestite... I thought, easy enough, I only need to wear a bra and a dress; nice of him to ask me."

*Before Night Falls* required Depp to take on two strongly contrasting roles, as the transvestite prisoner Bon Bon (above) and the sadistic guard Lieutenant Victor (right).

Opposite: Having made his name as an artist, Julian Schnabel has since proved equally adept as a director. His other critical successes include *Basquiat* (1996) and *The Diving Bell and the Butterfly* (2007).

As a new father, Johnny Depp made the conscious decision to seek out, for a while, smaller roles that would restrict his separation from his new family to the briefest possible periods. One of Depp's most intriguing projects from this time is *Before Night Falls*, a film that's based on the acclaimed, posthumously published 1993 autobiography of that name, by gay Cuban writer/dissident Reinaldo Arenas. This was the second movie directed by hard-charging, Falstaffian visual artist Julian Schnabel, who in 1996 won

over skeptical critics with his inventive and stylish (if heavily romanticized) debut *Basquiat*, a biopic about Jean-Michel Basquiat, the late New York graffiti artist whose naïve paintings made him an art-world sensation in the 1980s. Depp, who called Schnabel to congratulate him for *Basquiat* when the film was released, has pithily summed up the Brooklyn-born gadfly as "a witty guy, even if all his droll stories are about himself."

Several years after *Basquiat* Schnabel called Depp to ask whether he'd be interested in acting in *Before Night Falls*;

the actor would be taking on two cameo roles, the more striking of these being Bon Bon, a flamboyant transvestite whom Arenas encountered during one of his many spells in Havana's grim El Morro prison on politically motivated charges. (The real Reinaldo Arenas was one of the approximately 125,000 Cuban "undesirables" who were permitted to leave the island in the "Mariel boatlift" of 1980. The writer ended up in New York City, where he committed suicide in 1990, aged 47, three years after being diagnosed as HIV positive.)

Shedding whatever degree of Hollywood ego he may have possessed, Depp paid his own way to the film's Mexican location and threw himself headlong into his two minor, non-paying roles—despite the fact that it takes up only a few minutes of screen time, the actor's ultra-femme turn as Bon Bon had a greater impact than many of the mild-mannered leading men who are scattered across his résumé. Strutting around the prison yard as though he were to the stiletto born, Depp befriends the persecuted writer Arenas (played by Spanish actor Javier Bardem) and even smuggles out Arenas's manuscript in what seasoned prison-movie buffs refer to as "Papillon's wallet."

In his 1990 *Movieline* profile of Depp, Stephen Rebello quipped that the young actor has "the best cheekbones in Hollywood since Gene Tierney"—and in *Before Night Falls* Depp certainly imbued his drag queen with enough seedy glamor to get a few male filmgoers questioning their own sexuality. The second of the cameos that Schnabel handed to Depp was as one of Reinaldo Arenas's jailers, a sadistic official named Lieutenant Victor. Depp's portrayal of this scowling, slick haired, moustachioed monster—who, at one point, shoves a pistol into Arenas's mouth—clearly suggests that a strong current of repressed homosexuality is seething beneath the lieutenant's tight uniform. Two very different characters, but two sides of the same coin; and Depp's coin was a considerable gift to Schnabel's sophomore picture, proving that when he was in the mood the actor could achieve more in five minutes on screen than many peers could in five films.

Leading man Javier Bardem received an Academy Award nomination for his depiction of Arenas, while *Before Night Falls'* overwhelmingly positive notices gave a priceless boost to Julian Schnabel's stock as a director.

# Chocolat

2000

·················

"There are lots
of people out there
who are very good
at the 'boy meets girl,
boy loses girl, boy
finds girl again' stuff
and good luck
to them."

The charming *Chocolat* gave Johnny Depp another chance to act in a Lasse Hallström movie. With the actor's personal life having calmed down in the seven years since *What's Eating Gilbert Grape*, the Swedish director encountered a happier, healthier Depp this time around.

This project saw Johnny Depp reuniting with his *What's Eating Gilbert Grape* director Lasse Hallström, who had in the interim won an Oscar nomination for the 1999 romantic drama *The Cider House Rules* (adapted from John Irving's acclaimed novel of the same name and, like *Chocolat*, produced by indie-film titan Miramax Pictures). Depp later admitted that he had never actually seen *Gilbert Grape*, mainly because of his mental state while shooting the film in Austin, Texas. In a rare bout of self-revelation, the actor discussed his *Gilbert Grape* experience in at least one high-profile interview (although, as is his habit, he tended to skirt around the specifics of the situation).

"I was 30 when I made [*What's Eating Gilbert Grape*]," Depp told *Movieline* magazine. "It was a rough period for me, personally and emotionally, and when Lasse came to me with the idea of doing *Chocolat*, I was surprised he'd want to go through something with me again, thinking I was some kind of moody, brooding, horrible shithead."

Like *Gilbert Grape* and *The Cider House Rules*, *Chocolat* is adapted from a novel—in this case Joanne Harris's 1999 best-seller. And like Harris's book, Hallström's film is a devoutly middlebrow people-pleaser, in which the Swedish director offers sweet slabs of comfort food to the less adventurous devotee of foreign cinema. While the movie is set in France, subtitles are eschewed in favor of mildly accented English from the natives. The *New York Times* called *Chocolat* "an art-house movie for people who don't like art-house movies."

On his second collaboration with Lasse Hallström, Johnny Depp does not find himself having more or less to carry the entire film on his back, as was the case with *Gilbert Grape*. In *Chocolat* Depp—who drastically reduced his workload soon after the birth of his first child, Lily-Rose, in 1999—cedes center stage to the likes of Alfred Molina, Dame Judi Dench, and Juliette Binoche, all of whom have proved quite capable of carrying movies on their own when the occasion demanded it. So the fact that Depp is on screen for less than 20 minutes of

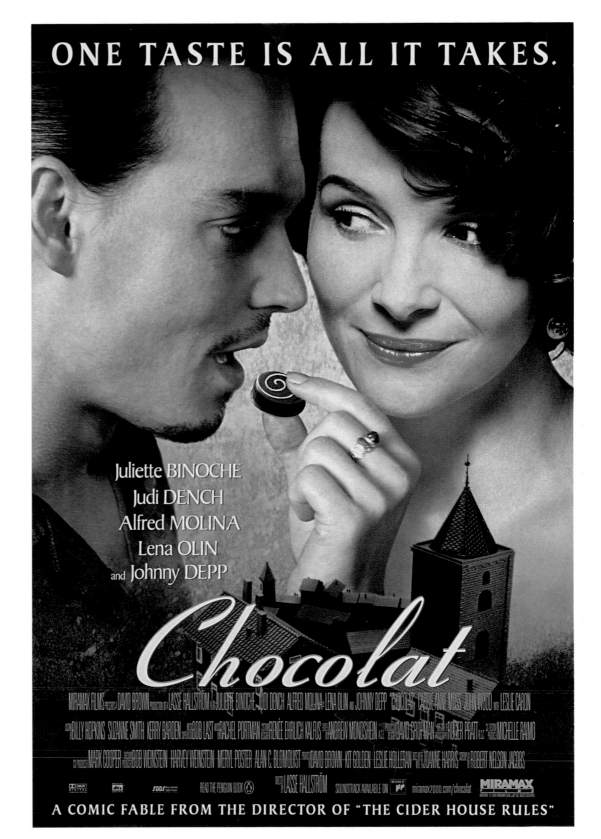

ONE TASTE IS ALL IT TAKES.

Juliette BINOCHE
Judi DENCH
Alfred MOLINA
Lena OLIN
and Johnny DEPP

*Chocolat*

A COMIC FABLE FROM THE DIRECTOR OF "THE CIDER HOUSE RULES"

*Chocolat*'s two-hour duration is far less of a loss than it would have been in just about any of his previous movies.

Leading lady Juliette Binoche plays a mysterious and beguiling free spirit named Vianne Rocher, who descends upon a conservative 1950s French town. Rocher, a single mother who's raising a pre-teen daughter on the road, throws civic decorum into chaos by opening up a coffee shop and selling handmade chocolates with properties that seemingly verge on the magical. Hallström's fanciful fable gets some much-needed ballast from its leading cast members, with Judi Dench giving yet another exemplary performance as a woman estranged from her daughter and thus deprived of any contact with her beloved grandson.

The redoubtable English character actor Alfred Molina turns in an agreeably comic performance as town mayor Comte Paul de Reynaud, a tightly wound prude who's incensed at the way in which this chocolate-hawking arriviste makes herself at home in his domain. Reynaud is a devout Catholic, and he regards Rocher—who happened to inaugurate her confectionery business during Lent—as a godless harridan who's having a malign, if not downright demonic, influence on his more malleable constituents.

> "*Chocolat was fun, but I'm not sure I'm particularly good at that sort of stuff. I'd probably be bored to tears if I had to do it all the time.*"

Reynaud is at least correct about Rocher's liberating effect on the locals, a theme which is at the soft center of *Chocolat*. Binoche's character uses her premises as a base for her informal work as a matchmaker, marriage counselor, women's-rights advocate, and all-round spiritual guru. Her secret weapon in all of this is her chocolate, and she carefully dispenses different varieties according to the personal needs of her customers. The fact that she opens for business on Sundays only confirms her place as Public Enemy Number One in the eyes of the mayor.

When a small armada of gypsy boats arrives at a nearby riverbank, its inhabitants provide a new focus for Reynaud's ire; and one of the gypsies ends up having a liberating effect on Vianne Rocher. This is, of course, Johnny Depp, as a languid, mildly raffish Irishman named Roux, who self-deprecatingly describes himself as a "river rat" when he first meets Rocher

almost an hour into the film. Depp pulls off a tolerable version of a polite Irish accent in his river-rat role, and even manages to wrest some competent blues licks from the acoustic guitar that accompanies him on his water-bound adventures. (It was former rock guitarist Depp who decided to give the character his musical proclivity.) In the overall narrative of *Chocolat*, this is a second-tier part that chiefly requires Depp to look—as they used to say—"windswept and interesting."

Roux, who has a young daughter of his own, effortlessly slips into a romantic relationship with Mlle Rocher, and even turns out to be a fairly useful handyman to have around the shop. However, a dim-witted local yokel interprets a passing remark by the mayor as an order to wage war on the visiting gypsy clan, and ends up torching one of their vessels. Exit Johnny Depp.

As "river rat" Roux, Depp falls for Vianne Rocher (Juliette Binoche).

Much to his own surprise and shame, Alfred Molina's repressive mayor ends up relenting, and gorging himself on one of Vianne Rocher's cocoa-based creations the day before Easter. Rocher placates her former enemy by agreeing not to reveal his messy secret. The film ends with Depp returning to the town to set up home with the Rocher family.

Despite its abundant sentimentality, *Chocolat* was generally very well received by critics, most of whom took the title as an open invitation to indulge in a warehouse's worth of confectionery-related metaphors. (*Time* magazine's Richard Schickel was among the refuseniks, and he upbraided Hallström for the film's "tasteful vulgarity.") As with a few of Depp's earlier works, the ever-reliable phrase "magical realism" was dusted off and used once again as a non-specific term for any film that doesn't quite make sense by traditional standards.

For once, Johnny Depp could remain happily oblivious to the reviews of one of his films, since his glorified cameo was barely even mentioned in dispatches. Still, it probably didn't hurt to be associated with any $25 million movie that could generate a truly remarkable $150 million in worldwide revenue. Apparently the market for cinematic comfort food was far bigger than anyone had imagined.

*Chocolat* may only be a slight if charming movie, but as a prestigious and highly profitable product of Miramax Pictures, it gave that company ample motivation to mount a strenuous Oscar campaign on its behalf. Although the film ultimately failed to garner any Academy Awards, its global financial success was gilded by an impressive five nominations—for best picture, actress, supporting actress, adapted screenplay, and original score.

# Blow

2001

·················

"I figured that my goal would be to take what seemed to be nothing but a party boy and turn him into a real man that you can relate to."

*"I felt a deep responsibility to George Jung because he's in a prison cell without the possibility of parole for a long time. I didn't get to spend that much time with him, but one day I just felt the character click into place. It's an exciting moment when you feel yourself thinking and moving and talking like another person."*

**C**ontrary to what people might think, I'm not 'Captain Weird', I just do what I do. The thing about making films is that it always has to be interesting, otherwise, why do it?" This was Johnny Depp's response in 2004, when he was asked for the three-thousandth time during an interview whether he chose his movie roles based on their "quirk" factor. With the generic drug-dealer saga *Blow*, Depp seemed to turn that question on its head: *OK, so this time Johnny's playing it dead straight… maybe that's the weirdest move of all!*

A ludicrous proposition, obviously—although it was still hard to comprehend exactly what an actor of Depp's stature was doing in what was basically a made-for-TV movie on steroids. *Blow* is based on the biography of fallen drug baron George Jung (played by Depp), and by depicting almost three decades of Jung's life "in the game," it tells a well-worn story in a very straightforward, linear fashion. Jung ends up losing everything and serving a lengthy prison sentence, but there is no moment of self-revelation from him, just as the film itself offers no real judgment of or new insight into the international drug business. Johnny Depp's fans get to see him wear an entertaining array of tacky retro fashions and enter into a doomed marriage with a hot-tempered Colombian chick played by Penélope Cruz.

At first glance it's easy to see what moved up-and-coming director Ted Demme (co-creator of the cable-TV phenomenon *Yo! MTV Raps*) to acquire the Jung biography for big-screen adaptation. George Jung was a Boston-born college dropout who found his true calling as a pot dealer, and ended up bringing planeloads of grass to the United States from Mexico. In 1974 he was arrested for smuggling over 600 pounds of marijuana and landed in federal prison in Connecticut: This sentence would turn out to be the biggest break of his life, because he befriended a fellow inmate named Carlos Lehder and tutored him in high-level smuggling.

Lehder happened to know Colombia's legendary cocaine kingpin Pablo Escobar, to whom he introduced Jung. Escobar (who was ultimately killed in a 1993 gun battle with Colombian police) decided to make the two friends his main importers of cocaine into the United States; before long the pair were said to be responsible for between 80 and 90 percent of the coke being sold in the country, which also made them largely responsible for the exploding popularity of the drug, which in 1985 was being used by over 20 million US citizens.

When Johnny Depp went to meet George Jung in prison before filming *Blow*, he found that Jung had no idea who he was. But when Jung ran Depp's name past fellow inmates, the actor met with their approval. "It's nice to know I'm liked in prison," Depp later quipped. Although the process of "aging" the actor over the decades was less than effective, Depp's surprisingly bland portrayal of Jung (in a film with a remarkable absence of comment on the drug trade) had the former millionaire felon saying that he felt as though the actor had stolen his soul.

Unfortunately, even the most compelling events in Jung's story already seemed overfamiliar to viewers; and since these events occur relatively early in Demme's picture, one is left with the distinct sense that George Jung's life can only go downhill thereafter. And indeed, the remainder of the picture plays out as a prolonged descent toward the inevitable arrest

Left: Cocaine smuggler
George Jung (Johnny Depp)
living the high life with
his Colombian wife Mirtha
(Penélope Cruz).

Above: An on-set discussion
with director Ted Demme.

of George Jung, who has been cast aside by his old prison buddy. The viewer could almost be forgiven for feeling a sense of relief when Jung's mother turns him over to the police after he skips bail—particularly in light of the fact that the protagonist's father is played by none other than Ray Liotta, the star of Martin Scorsese's *Goodfellas*, a movie that handled similar subject matter (and displayed a similar volume of garish polyester and bad leather) with infinitely greater style, substance, and nuance.

As if *Blow* didn't have enough inherent problems, the film was released in April 2001, in the wake of a much more ambitious and prestigious drug movie, Steven Soderbergh's star-laden *Traffic*. Although *Traffic* was little more than a melodramatic reduction of the three-part British TV drama (*Traffik*) on which it was based, the picture tackled its subject with sufficient gravitas to pick up four gold statues at that year's Academy Awards. Nonetheless, *Blow*—despite receiving largely tepid reviews—ultimately ended up being a modest commercial success in the US.

A bitter postscript was added to the movie when director Ted Demme died in January 2002 while playing basketball with friends. Toxicology reports found traces of cocaine in Demme's system, an acrid reminder of the plague George Jung had unleashed upon his own nation decades before.

# From Hell

2001

......................

"The appeal of a
film like *From Hell*
for me is that it
is pretty dark and
I've always been
interested in human
behavior."

**F**rom Hell began its life as a 10-part graphic-novel series written by Alan Moore, illustrated in black and white by Eddie Campbell, and published between 1991 and 1996. This was a grim and riveting saga that did not stint on the more gruesome realities of Victorian life as the fiercely intelligent Moore presented a new, complex, and highly nuanced theory about the notoriously barbaric serial-killer Jack the Ripper, who terrorized the East End of London between 1888 and 1891. The writer's fundamental thesis is that one of Queen Victoria's grandsons, Prince Albert Victor, Duke of Clarence (who lived, according to his grandma, a "dissipated" life), fathered a child by an East End prostitute. Moore alleges that the Queen dispatched the prominent surgeon William Gill to locate the harlot in question, and to seriously damage her memory by any means necessary.

Gill duly complies with Her Majesty's callous command, and then diligently sets about murdering a number of other streetwalkers who may have been aware of Albert's illegitimate child. The doctor brings a messianic zeal to his task, and the brutal and ritualistic nature of his crimes sends shockwaves across the British capital. Moore and Campbell's award-winning saga places these despicable acts firmly within the context of the economic strife and hegemonic politics that prevailed in late nineteenth-century Britain; significantly enough, the movie adaptation does no such thing.

The film rights to From Hell were acquired in 1996 by a division of the Walt Disney Company for just under $2 million, but the property spent several years in limbo before Twentieth Century Fox took it on, handing a budget of over $30 million to co-directors Albert and Allen Hughes. These Detroit-born twin brothers were widely regarded as black filmmakers, despite their bi-racial provenance; before making From Hell, they had directed two feature films and one documentary, all of which dealt with specifically black subject matter.

> *"I've been fascinated by [Jack the Ripper] since I was a young kid. I jumped at the chance to do the film. It meant I could talk to some of the great Ripperologists and I got to wander through the area of Whitechapel at night. I loved that."*

In *From Hell* Depp plays Inspector Frederick Abberline, a detective who has his own secrets to hide while investigating the Jack the Ripper murders.

Johnny Depp expressed strong interest in playing the film's chief protagonist, Inspector Frederick Abberline, the real-life police officer who led the investigation into the Ripper murders. Depp has admitted to having a lifelong fascination with Jack the Ripper, which began when he came across a PBS Ripper documentary at the age of eight. "Nothing like this had ever happened before on such a grand scale and before the world's eyes," Depp told one interviewer for a Canadian newspaper. "And the most fascinating thing about it is that it's still unsolved and it certainly seems pretty guaranteed that it will always be unsolved." The actor admitted to having read virtually all the major books written about Jack the Ripper, and said that the central hypothesis of *From Hell* was "by no means far-fetched."

Depp was duly cast as Frederick Abberline, obliging the film's screenwriters, Terry Hayes and Rafael Yglesias, significantly to reduce the age of the real Abberline, and disregard his morose temperament. The two writers made countless changes to Moore and Campbell's original story, the most significant of which was probably their depiction of Abberline as a high-functioning opium addict who, while under the drug's influence, has premonitions of future murders. (The 2002 Steven Spielberg thriller *Minority Report* placed the controlled, pre-emptive use of similar visions in a sci-fi context.) Any adaptation of a 10-part series into a two-hour motion picture is bound to involve a great deal of original material being discarded, but Hayes and Yglesias also added so many new elements that their final adaptation of *From Hell* was probably worthy of a new title.

For anyone who—unlike the Hughes brothers and their writers—has even a passing familiarity with Victorian London and the still-unsolved Ripper case, *From Hell* offered only the slimmest of pickings. Johnny Depp's performance measured up to his own high standards, and his London accent even drew praise from several British critics. Most of the film's highlights involve Depp's erudite verbal jousting with rotund

*"In terms of hero, anti-hero, reluctant hero, whatever, for me, Abberline was an interesting opportunity to play a dedicated police inspector who was not only dealing with the demon of Jack the Ripper and that mystery, but he was dealing with his own demons at the same time."*

"I didn't mean it as business." Prostitute Mary Kelly (Heather Graham) attempts to kiss Abberline, who resists at first but then succumbs.

Overleaf: Portrait by Jérôme De Perlinghi, 2001.

colleague Sergeant Peter Godley (played by the Scottish actor Robbie Coltrane, of *Harry Potter* fame). Overall, though, the Hughes brothers opted to turn the original *From Hell* into a more straightforward whodunnit populated by stock period archetypes who inhabited the kind of quaint, imaginary London that wouldn't even have spooked Dick Van Dyke. When it came to handing out the film's many prostitute roles, the film's casting directors adroitly identified a group of English character actresses whose raw-boned and vaguely malnourished looks credibly conveyed the cruel depredations of Victorian London. But their most prominent colleague, Mary Kelly, is played by Heather Graham, the epitome of a corn-fed, fluoridated modern American who—presumably in between back-alley shifts— ends up providing some Hollywood-style love interest for the supposedly stoic Inspector Abberline. Graham's presence is

enough to throw the film further off balance, and her fitful grasp of the English accent puts the entire edifice in grave danger.

When *From Hell* was released on DVD in 2002, the disc's audio commentary revealed that Fox harbored some serious doubts about this picture—but these predominantly concerned the casting of Johnny Depp in the role of Inspector Abberline. The studio did not question Depp's acting prowess, or his proven ability to handle a foreign accent—like many of their colleagues throughout the industry, Fox's top executives suspected that the actor's capricious approach to choosing his film roles was seriously undermining his appeal as a leading man. They should perhaps have focused their concerns on other aspects of the production, because with Depp on board, *From Hell*—despite all the aforementioned flaws—went on to earn a very respectable $75 million worldwide.

*I'm not sure what's scarier, commercial failure
or commercial success."*

# Pirates of the Caribbean
## The Curse of the Black Pearl

2003

"When a little kid approaches me on the street and screams, 'Hey, you're that Captain Jack Sparrow!' then I am always deeply touched."

DEPP          RUSH          BLOOM          KNIGHTLEY

A JERRY BRUCKHEIMER PRODUCTION

# Pirates of the Caribbean
## THE CURSE OF THE BLACK PEARL

WALT DISNEY PICTURES PRESENTS IN ASSOCIATION WITH JERRY BRUCKHEIMER FILMS JOHNNY DEPP GEOFFREY RUSH "PIRATES OF THE CARIBBEAN: THE CURSE OF THE BLACK PEARL" A GORE VERBINSKI FILM
ORLANDO BLOOM KEIRA KNIGHTLEY AND JONATHAN PRYCE MUSIC SUPERVISOR BOB BADAMI MUSIC BY ALAN SILVESTRI VISUAL EFFECTS AND ANIMATION BY INDUSTRIAL LIGHT & MAGIC COSTUME DESIGNER PENNY ROSE
EDITED BY CRAIG WOOD STEPHEN RIVKIN, A.C.E. ARTHUR R. SCHMIDT DIRECTOR OF PHOTOGRAPHY DARIUSZ WOLSKI, A.S.C. EXECUTIVE PRODUCERS MIKE STENSON CHAD OMAN BRUCE HENDRICKS PAUL DEASON
PIRATESMOVIES.COM PRODUCED BY JERRY BRUCKHEIMER SCREENPLAY BY TED ELLIOTT & TERRY ROSSIO AND JAY WOLPERT DIRECTED BY GORE VERBINSKI

*"Who wouldn't want to play a pirate? When I was first offered the role, I thought it was a joke. Why would Disney want to cast me? I was more shocked than anyone."*

When an October 2000 article in *Variety* noted that Walt Disney Studios, under new chairman Peter Schneider, was in the process of developing several major motion pictures based on its company's theme-park rides—including the "audio-animatronic" attraction "Pirates of the Caribbean"—the news caused nary a ripple of interest within the Hollywood community. A few eyebrows may have been raised the following year when Disney announced that action-movie titan Jerry Bruckheimer, who'd recently forged an unlikely alliance with the studio, would be in charge of its inauspicious-sounding pirate project. But when the company announced in 2002 that Johnny Depp would be taking the lead role in *Pirates of the Caribbean: The Curse of the Black Pearl*, Hollywood was practically engulfed in a tidal wave of astonishment.

And no one was more shocked at this bizarre development than… Johnny Depp. The actor happened to be meeting with one of Disney's top executives to discuss potential future collaborations, and mentioned that "I'd like to do some kiddie stuff," with his own young offspring in mind. No sooner had the Disney "suit" brought up the company's plans for a "Pirates" film than Depp blurted out, "I'm in!"

Months later the actor was still trying to figure out exactly why he'd made this impetuous decision, which seemed to directly violate just about every artistic principle he had ever espoused. "I can't explain it, you know," said Depp, who was paid $14 million to work on the movie. "I just had a feeling. And there was every chance in the world for it to be something horribly embarrassing."

Quite so. Every major Hollywood studio had steered well clear of anything skull-and-crossbones related since 1995, when the Finnish action-movie director Renny Harlin cast his then girlfriend Geena Davis as the lead in *Cutthroat Island*, the supposedly rollicking tale of a fearless female pirate. Once Harlin had imposed his single-minded vision on every single aspect of the production, his completed movie was a hyperkinetic, rudderless mess that became a box-office flop of mythical proportions, failing to recoup one tenth of its $115 million budget on its way to Davy Jones' Video Locker.

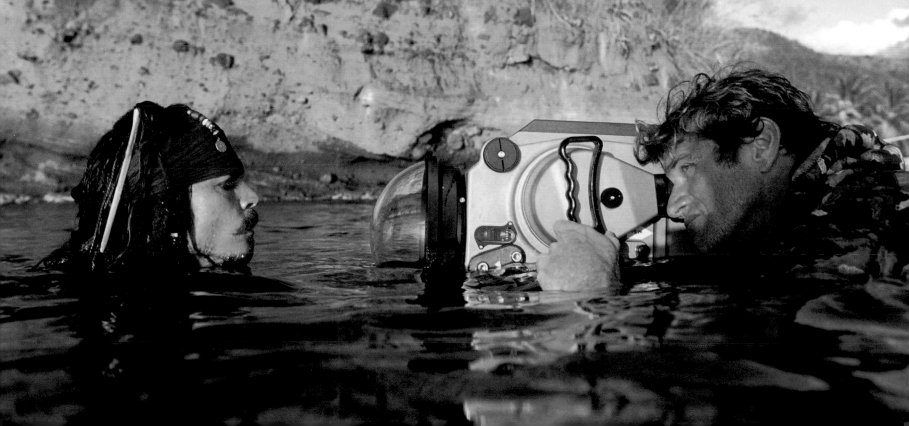

*"Every character you play has parts of you in it, and there's some of me in Captain Jack. But now there's probably more of Captain Jack in me. He won't leave me alone. He showed up this morning as I was getting my kids ready for school, but I managed to shoo him away."*

Marooned on a desert island with nothing for company but a cache of rum and governor's daughter Elizabeth Swann (Keira Knightley).

Then again, whenever a movie genre seems to have been killed stone dead, there usually remains the possibility that it might be reincarnated at a later date, with a combination of the perfect project and even better timing. In this instance, it was Johnny Depp's unheralded *Pirates of the Caribbean* that got millions of people peppering their conversation with bits of arcane pirate parlance.

*Pirates* director Gore Verbinski may not have been ranked as an A-list talent at the time, but he'd already proved himself a versatile young journeyman with the 1997 kiddie-comedy hit *Mousehunt*, the middling Brad Pitt/Julia Roberts vehicle *The Mexican* (2001), and *The Ring*, a phenomenally successful 2002 re-make of the 1998 Japanese psychological horror movie. As it turned out, Verbinski and his leading man struck up the kind of personal affinity that can make the difference between a happy and productive working relationship and another day at the office: The two men were both born in the American south (in Verbinski's case, Tennessee), and both had served time in

punk-influenced rock bands before gravitating toward the movie business. The pair therefore shared the kind of sensibility and sense of humor that was clearly manifested when Verbinski first saw Depp's visual interpretation of his character, a most unusual pirate by the name of Captain Jack Sparrow. As the whole world now knows, this involved copious amounts of eyeliner, a red bandana, gold teeth, beaded beard-braids, plus a mop of quasi-dreadlocks weighed down by countless little trinkets of great significance to the battle-scarred seaman. "Gore came in, looked, and said, 'Yeah, that's it,'" Depp recalls. "He supported it, he understood it, and he got the humor."

The Disney executives came in, looked, and nearly had a heart attack about what might happen to their $140 million investment in the hands of this decadent creature. Bruckheimer recalls getting the following impression of Disney's attitude when its corporate overlords visited the set: "What are they doing? They've got a pirate with mascara on!" Depp was prepared to walk the plank for the integrity of his bizarre

*"For a guy like me, who's been dangling in this business for the last 20 years, to finally have something hit, it's unexpected and very touching."*

This page and overleaf: Inspired by Keith Richards, Depp's sun-addled buccaneer gets himself in—and out—of all manner of perilous situations throughout the movie's 143-minute running time.

There are superficial similarities, of course, although Gore Verbinski was hell-bent on capturing the filth-encrusted reality of the pirate milieu. But despite the impressive list of names among *Pirates'* supporting cast, it is Depp's Captain Jack Sparrow who keeps your eyes glued to the screen whenever he's up there. Will he win his ongoing, *Looney Tunes*-style war with gravity? Is the man an idiot or a savant—or some kind of shaman? Is he stoned, drunk, or just severely sun-addled? And how on earth does he manage to keep firing off all those insouciant bons mots even when there's some scurvy-ridden blackguard pressing a razor-sharp sword against his windpipe?

Which is not to suggest that *Pirates of the Caribbean: The Curse of the Black Pearl* is merely a series of roped-together Jack Sparrow set pieces. Depp's character just happens to be the pivotal figure in a rambunctious, convoluted, and oddly enthralling story that involves a rival pirate named Barbossa (played with maximum relish by Geoffrey Rush) who's stolen Sparrow's ship, and is on a desperate quest to find and return the final piece of stolen Aztec gold that will rid him and his men of a curse that makes them morph into fleshless ghouls during any full moon.

We first see Depp stepping off the mast of a sinking ship and sauntering onto a pier on Port Royal, Jamaica, where he will encounter the accursed Barbossa. In a misguided attempt to recover his gold, the latter kidnaps Elizabeth Swann, daughter of the island's governor and (as played by the English ingenue Keira Knightley) nobody's pushover. A childhood friend of Elizabeth's, the sword maker Will Turner (played somewhat incongruously by the willowy Orlando Bloom), persuades Jack

Sparrow to give chase in a purloined British navy vessel, which is in turn followed by HMS *Dauntless*, under the command of Elizabeth's fiancé, the rigid-backed Commodore Norrington.

Although Captain Jack's sentience seems to be questionable throughout the subsequent romp across high seas, he will always snap into full consciousness at the sound of a sword being drawn from its scabbard; at which point the good Captain resembles some louche and ironic reincarnation of every great Hollywood pirate, from Errol Flynn to Douglas Fairbanks Jr. And, as with *Ed Wood*, Depp never feels the need to let the audience know that he is "in" on the joke. Playing it dead straight is just one component of a performance that is, as they say, "better than it has to be"; or in this case, better than it has a right to be.

As the June 2003 Disneyland launch of *Pirates of the Caribbean: The Curse of the Black Pearl* approached, there was very little expectation surrounding a movie that was generally regarded as a freakish hybrid with no particular relevance to modern cinema. Among the industry folk who'd attended *Pirates*

screenings, however, the more perceptive viewers came away with the distinct sense that they may have just seen something very special. Even so, no one would have predicted that the bastard offspring of Depp and Disney would soon be pillaging its way into the record books as a $3 billion worldwide cultural phenomenon that has spawned (to date) three money-spinning sequels, and allowed Johnny Depp to purchase his own private island in the Caribbean. (The first *Pirates* film earned $300 million in the US and $350 million abroad.)

In such situations movie critics' opinions tend to become devalued to the point of irrelevance, and this one was no different. However, going through the reviews of the first *Pirates* movie is a mildly entertaining exercise, if only because of the confusion Depp managed to create. A few critics grumbled about the film's 143-minute length, but most verdicts tended to be on the positive side, and of course Depp was not short-changed in the kudos department. (The film also brought him an Oscar nomination.) But the odd thing is how few reviewers allowed themselves to experience the sheer sensory pleasure of

the whole thing, which is after all the reason audiences came to see the film in such numbers.

The importance of Johnny Depp's role to *Pirates*'s box-office triumph has been a matter of some debate since the film's opening weekend in July 2003, and as with any other discussion about movies there can never be a definite conclusion. But judging by his effusive praise for Depp, his Oscar-winning *Pirates* co star Geoffrey Rush seemed to be in little doubt about the issue. "It was extraordinary to see Johnny create this character," said Rush. "It was such a cool performance very masterfully done. He is a brilliant actor."

Of all Depp's Hollywood peers, Robert Downey Jr. is perhaps the only one fit to kiss one of Captain Jack's numerous rings: One could argue that the *Iron Man* and *Sherlock Holmes* movies owe most of their phenomenal worldwide success to Downey's ability to create two distinct, equally memorable leading men who are every bit as contradictory and feckless as Johnny Depp's Captain Jack. But it is no slight on Downey's quicksilver presence to suggest that he probably lacks one vital component

that Depp still brings to the table: sex appeal. Given that *People* magazine in 2003 bestowed upon Depp its famously dubious honor "The Sexiest Man Alive," it's safe to say that, even as he approached the age of 40, Depp still retained the same genetic gifts that landed him on *21 Jump Street* back in the late eighties, and that the defining moment of his mercurial career came when he found a character that would let him combine his classic film-star looks with every bit of craft, wit, and inventiveness he'd accrued over the previous decades.

It's hardly unusual to see a film star being showered with "I knew him when" encomiums after one of his movies cleans up at the box office; however, Harvey Weinstein, the co-founder of the indie-film powerhouse Miramax, and then the Weinstein Company, is not generally one to gush about anything he did not invest in. But in the wake of the first *Pirates* film, the ursine executive seemed intent on settling some scores for Johnny Depp. "He's been frozen out for years," said Weinstein. "He was looked at as too risky for a lot of the top stuff. A lot of people are going to be kissing his butt now."

# Once Upon a Time in Mexico

2003

.....................

"Here was a chance to play a guy who was a little against the grain of what you'd expect to see in a CIA agent."

Left: Devious CIA agent Sheldon Sands (Johnny Depp) tangles with the double-crossing Ajedrez (Eva Mendes).

Opposite right: Almost certainly the only sighting of a Judy Garland biography in a Spaghetti Western.

The only film Johnny Depp made in the calendar year 2001 was *Once Upon a Time in Mexico*, the third part of the "Mariachi" trilogy by his writer/director friend Robert Rodriguez. (The first two parts were *El Mariachi* from 1992 [which earned $2 million in the US despite its $200,000 micro-budget] and *Desperado* from 1995, which—like *Once Upon a Time*—featured Antonio Banderas as Mariachi, the existentialist gunslinger hero of the first movie.) Depp was booked for only nine days of shooting in June 2001, but he reportedly enjoyed the experience so much that he implored Rodriguez to give him a second, minor cameo role before he flew back to Paris. Depp even composed and recorded a musical theme for his character, which Rodriguez actually ended up using in the film.

The part Johnny Depp had been hired to play was, for any actor with a modicum of proficiency, the proverbial low-hanging fruit: a corrupt and amoral CIA agent named Sheldon Sands, a man so loathed within his own agency that he gets himself banished to a flea-bitten Mexican hellhole—the kind of place, as it happens, in which Robert Rodriguez likes to set his "Mariachi" movies.

Although the cast of *Once Upon a Time* contains two inveterate scenery-chewers in Willem Dafoe and Mickey Rourke, it's young Johnny Depp who steals the limelight at every opportunity, and who raises the picture to the level of an almost-respectable Spaghetti Western. (On this occasion Johnny Depp took just an individual model for the irredeemable spook Sands: a sadly unnamed Hollywood executive whose vile machinations had left the actor speechless when they worked together.)

But whereas the original Spaghetti Westerns—as pioneered in the mid-sixties by Italian director Sergio Leone—tended to be gritty, straight-shooting moral fables, Rodriguez seemed intent on making his movie as dense and convoluted as possible. In formal terms, he elects to employ in-jokey "flashbacks" from an imaginary "third" Mariachi picture that is supposed to exist in some temporal black hole between *Desperado* and *Once Upon a Time*. Johnny Depp is clearly having as much fun as anyone involved as he practically dares us not to despise the lawless CIA man Sands (who, at Depp's suggestion, uses a false third arm in certain scenes). Then again, as Rodriguez later remarked, "I don't think you can really hate a Johnny Depp character, no matter how rotten he may be."

The film's storyline goes for baroque, with Sands getting caught up in elaborate deals with drug cartels, abortive coup attempts and a spiraling vortex of betrayal that ends up with him

being blinded—but still determined to face his enemy in a pistol duel. With a touch of typically mordant, and sporadically redeeming humor, Rodriguez shows Sands being led toward his face-off by a small boy.

Although Rodriguez gamely packs his Byzantine shoot-'em-up with as much sound and fury as any movie could handle, *Once Upon a Time* is ultimately a blood-soaked baffler that ends up failing to signify much at all. And the critics did not hesitate to point this out to the movie's director: *Newsweek*'s John Anderson described Rodriguez's latest effort as "a movie that goes so wrong so abruptly it's as if a meteor were heading for the set and everyone had to evacuate." Anderson had to admit, however, that this cosmic train-wreck of a film still did have at least one thing going for it: the Depp Factor.

*Once Upon a Time* was made extremely quickly by contemporary Hollywood standards, thanks largely to Rodriguez's prescient use of digital cameras; since these devices also eliminate the cost of film, a director can shoot as many hours of footage as he sees fit. Which sounds like something approaching total creative freedom until one considers the exponential increase in the number of editing-room decisions facing the director when it comes time to compress a vast choice of takes down to the sub-120 minute length of a standard feature film. This process may have been one of the factors that kept *Once Upon a Time in Mexico* from reaching theaters until September 2003—over two years after filming ended. This turned out to be a most serendipitous delay, given that the movie landed in theaters just a few short weeks after *Pirates of the Caribbean* had ratified Depp's status as an International Movie Star. Robert Rodriguez spent $29 million on making a movie that earned over $55 million domestically and over $30 million overseas. Whenever a film makes such a tidy profit, no one minds if the critics want to quibble about how messy the plot is.

# Secret Window

2004

·····················

"It's always great
to get in the ring with
actors you respect.
But when you're in
there by yourself, it's
quite challenging."

"What I remember most was reading the screenplay. I got 10 to 15 pages into it and thought, 'Wow, this is incredibly well written. The dialogue is real and not forced, with an interesting train of thought quality to it.'"

Left: Fine-tuning with director David Koepp, who also wrote the screenplay for this adaptation of a Stephen King novella. Depp plays renowned mystery writer Mort Rainey whose life disintegrates when he is confronted with a ghost from his own past.

Another Johnny Depp curveball—the kind of film that leaves you wondering, "Is this man so rich and famous that he can use the *I Ching* to make major career decisions?" Which is not to say that there's anything remotely distasteful about this tidy little suspense thriller, which also features the redoubtable talents of actors like John Turturro, Maria Bello, and Timothy Hutton, as well as writer/director David Koepp, whose previous experience included penning screenplays for global blockbusters such as *Jurassic Park*, *Spider-Man*, and *Indiana Jones and the Kingdom of the Crystal Skull*. *Secret Window* was only the third movie Koepp had directed, so perhaps he was looking for a safe bet when he opted to adapt a Stephen King novella, which was published with the title *Secret Window, Secret Garden*.

Perhaps it's Johnny Depp's apparent disinclination—with the obvious exception of *Dead Man*—to dabble in anything that might appear remotely distasteful that makes this prosaic subcategory of his work so baffling. We are, after all, talking about an actor who has for some time possessed the type of cultural equity that usually grants its owner an enviable level of artistic autonomy that will be withdrawn only if he switches off his brain and puts his career on autopilot. One of the most curious things about the media-friendly yet ultimately reticent Depp is the way he'll drift into a project as inauspicious as, say, *Nick of Time* because he feels some inexplicable affinity with the script; then there is his recurring and somewhat perverse desire to play "the ordinary guy," the kind of faceless salaryman whom he imagines "putting out the Water Wiggle in the backyard for his kid."

Like most of Depp's journeyman detours, *Secret Window* clearly belongs to a time-tested genre; in this case, the type of film that leads us to question a protagonist's version of "reality," then ultimately attempts to trip us up with some final "revelation" or twist. Such endeavors become less appealing by the year, because they are playing to an audience whose unprecedented access to, and awareness of, genre pictures gives the movies' creators the unenviable task of trying to remain perpetually at least one thought ahead of the "hive mind." (One could call this state of affairs "the M. Night Shyamalan conundrum.")

The advertising posters for *Secret Window* are dominated by a head-shot of the erstwhile Captain Jack Sparrow, who wears a look of great consternation as well as a neat goatee and a pair of black-rimmed glasses that clearly connote a Man of Letters. The character in question goes by the name of Mort Raincy, and is a popular horror/crime novelist who's finalizing a divorce while slouching around his remote cabin in a shabby dressing gown, trying to overcome a chronic case of writer's block. Rainey's smoke-cured solipsism is disturbed one day by a visit from a passive-aggressive hick with the subtly disquieting name John Shooter (played by John Turturro as though he had been in cold storage since his role in 2000 in *O Brother, Where Art Thou?*). The unctuous interloper hands Rainey an old manuscript; supposed proof that one of Rainey's stories was plagiarized, word for word, from something Shooter wrote years earlier. He demands restitution.

Despite the tasteful Philip Glass score that chimes in the background, things take a turn for the formulaic as Rainey tries to disprove Shooter's accusation. The writer becomes more and more unhinged, until his soon-to-be ex-wife Amy (Maria Bello) starts to become seriously concerned—per genre stipulation—about his mental state. Of course, her female intuition is proven right by a rapidly unfolding sequence of events that viewers either regarded as horrific and alarming or downright risible.

*Secret Window* might have been acceptable as a single episode of a 1960s mystery series like *The Twilight Zone* or *The Outer Limits*, but critics were happy to point out all the ways in which David Koepp's film fell short of contemporary standards. And once again—per media stipulation—Johnny Depp was found not guilty of the numerous charges that were leveled against the project as a whole, and in fact received a fair amount of praise for his contribution.

Despite his habit of keeping his emotional drawbridge up during interviews, Depp will occasionally reveal a brief glimpse of one, apparently genuine personality trait that sets him apart from most of the entertainers in his tax bracket: honesty. During the launch of *Secret Window*, he talked the film up by offering more or less the same conclusion that its many critics drew. "It's classic Stephen King," said Depp. "And then you suddenly go: 'Oh crap! Are you kidding?'"

# Happily Ever After

2004

· · · · · · · · · · · · · · · · · · ·

"I feel much more
comfortable in Europe.
You know there's a huge
difference. I will never
understand the animal,
the machine of Hollywood.
The beast of it all. I don't
want to understand it."

claude berri présente

charlotte gainsbourg — yvan attal
alain chabat — emmanuelle seigner — alain cohen

# ils se marièrent
## et eurent beaucoup d'enfants
un film de yvan attal

aurore clément angie david
avec la participation de anouk aimée
scénario et dialogues yvan attal image remy chevrin A.F.C
son didier sain jean goudier jean-paul hurier marc doisne
montage jennifer augé décors katia wyszkop costumes jacqueline bouchard
producteur associé nathalie rheims producteur exécutif pierre grunstein directeur de production nicole firn
une coproduction hirsch - pathé renn production - TF1 films production
avec la participation de canal + et du centre national de la cinématographie

Left: The French poster for *Ils Se Marièrent et Eurent Beaucoup d'Enfants*.

Below: On set in Paris during the filming of *Happily Ever After*, a French movie by Yvan Attal in which Depp plays L'Inconnu (The Unknown).

Opposite: Gabrielle (Charlotte Gainsbourg) is transfixed by the handsome stranger she encounters while listening to the same Radiohead track in a record store.

Previous page: At a press conference in Toronto, shortly after the film's release.

The inexorable rise of the *Pirates of the Caribbean* franchise earned Johnny Depp a degree of personal autonomy even higher than the one he'd doggedly acquired over the course of nearly two decades as a recalcitrant "character actor in the body of a leading man." Thus we find this curio among his oeuvre: an independent French-language film to which the newly anointed global megastar lends his towering cultural equity for a grand total of two scenes.

*Happily Ever After* is helmed by the Israeli-born actor/director Yvan Attal, father of three children with the film's star Charlotte Gainsbourg, daughter of French cultural icon Serge, and an acquaintance of Depp's from the world of jet-set bohemia. Attal's movie adroitly examines the vagaries of modern married life by focusing on a handful of interconnected couples, the most prominent of whom are named Gabrielle and Vincent (Gainsbourg and Attal himself). Depp—whose character is billed as "L'Inconnu" (The Unknown)—is not under examination here; in fact he is used only as a cipher of sorts.

186

He first appears in the film after almost 18 minutes, when he sidles up next to the saturnine Gabrielle at a listening booth in the enormous Virgin Megastore on the Champs-Élysées in Paris. The short episode that ensues is a minor masterpiece of social discomfort, with Gainsbourg getting increasingly flustered each time she looks over at the handsome young professional standing a few feet away, seemingly oblivious to her gaze. The scene would have played perfectly well without sound, but the director elects to drown it in the sound of "Creep," Radiohead's overwrought anthem of self-loathing.

L'Inconnu smiles convivially and departs with CD in hand. After a moment's hesitation Gabrielle scrambles desperately through the throng of shoppers in pursuit of this chimerical looker with the floppy, blond-streaked hair. She finds him idly browsing in another section of the store, but she's too nervous to speak; L'Inconnu breaks the ice by smiling genially and holding up his CD purchase. She responds by awkwardly showing him the same item. Gabrielle takes her musical purchase back to a

less than idyllic household, where husband Vincent plays a crude practical joke on her as she bathes their young son.

Gabrielle's days are spent in a state of enervation as she juggles endless calls in a realtor's office. Toward the end of the film we see her arranging to show another apartment to another client. As she waits in front of the building, The Velvet Underground's jittery classic "I'm Waiting for the Man" plays in the foreground. "The Man," of course, turns out to be Johnny Depp, with whom Gabrielle briefly chats, first in French, then in English. He asks whether they might have met before, but Gabrielle demurs. They enter the building and board a tiny, old-fashioned elevator for an ascent so prolonged as to suggest a building as tall as the Tour Eiffel. As clouds suddenly encircle the pair, we appear to be entering Gabrielle's mid-air romantic fantasy. Thankfully Yvan Attal resists the temptation to blast out Aerosmith's ham-fisted "Love in an Elevator" as the couple turn toward each other; they kiss to the sound of lush mid-century muzak. Fade to black.

# Finding Neverland

2004

...................

"I think the idea of
staying a child forever
is beautiful, and I
think you can."

On set with director Marc
Forster, Kate Winslet, and
Joe Prospero.

Peter Llewelyn Davies
(Freddie Highmore) rejects his
pirate name, "Dastardly Jim."

*"It's so good to be working in London again. Living in Paris, London is the nearest place I can work without that Hollywood crap."*

After Miramax Pictures announced its plans to adapt Allan Knee's successful stage play *The Man Who Was Peter Pan* as the feature film *Finding Neverland*, there was a widespread belief that the new project was bound to haul in a sackful of Oscar nominations. Director Marc Forster's previous outing, *Monster's Ball*, was an independent production that garnered one Academy Award and one nomination in 2002; Kate Winslet, *Finding Neverland*'s leading lady, was an established industry darling who had been nominated four times before she turned 30. Then, of course, there was Johnny Depp, who'd be appearing in the role of Scottish writer J.M. Barrie, creator of the evergreen hit play *Peter Pan*.

*Finding Neverland* looked like exactly the kind of genteel British period drama for which Academy voters have a notorious soft spot—then there was the fearsome publicity machine that Miramax (then owned by Disney) would annually unleash upon the general public and, more specifically, Academy voters in

the run-up to the Oscars. Given the impressive combination of elements connected to *Finding Neverland*, this movie was not regarded as one of Miramax's hardest-ever Oscar sells.

The film depicts the haphazard conception and creation of *Peter Pan*, a work that contemporary Hollywood probably knows best as one of the money-spinning animated perennials to which Disney periodically gives a limited release on DVD. The industry was also beginning to recognize Johnny Depp as a formidable box-office attraction, thanks to the phenomenal global success of his 2003 Disney film, *Pirates of the Caribbean: The Curse of the Black Pearl*. After playing that movie's franchise-defining character, Captain Jack Sparrow, Depp made the eminently sensible decision that this was the moment to put aside his pirate's costume and outré behavior in favor of itchy wool suits and a crisp Scottish accent.

So what could possibly go wrong? Let us start with David Magee's screen adaptation of Allan Knee's stage play, which

somehow managed to weigh down the first two-thirds of the movie with rather ponderous pacing. It's not uncommon to see movies that begin promisingly, then lose their way after an hour or so, so it's surprising when a picture goes in the opposite direction: *Finding Neverland* starts off with something of a whimper and ends—emotionally speaking—with a bang. Although Magee dispenses with several significant elements and characters from the stage play in the interests of expedience, he does not establish the remaining characters quickly or strongly enough, or convincingly define the relationships between them.

Depp's J.M. Barrie is a playwright whose most recent West End play, *Little Mary*, was an abject failure, and who is consequently under pressure from his agent (played by Dustin Hoffman, in a piquant cameo) to write a bona fide hit. The Scotsman has long been trapped in a loveless marriage that prompts him to focus his attention away from the family home whenever possible; not to mention the fact that it does precious

little for his confidence as a writer. One day, while walking his dog in a London park, Barrie has a random encounter with the attractive widow Sylvia Llewelyn Davies (the typically peerless Winslet) and her four young sons. The playwright entertains the lads by acting out all manner of fanciful tales, and then charmingly inveigles his way into the bosom of the family—although it's made perfectly clear that Barrie has no such designs on the ample bosom of Winslet's character. This is just as well, since we soon enough discover that Mrs. Llewelyn Davies is suffering from tuberculosis, and is thus unlikely to be around when the movie's closing titles roll.

If you've ever wondered why certain actors claim to avoid reading their own notices, the tendency might be partially explained by one particular review of *Finding Neverland*. When the film was critiqued in one British broadsheet, the writer took issue with Depp's Scottish accent, peevishly suggesting that it brought to mind a working-class Glaswegian rather than a

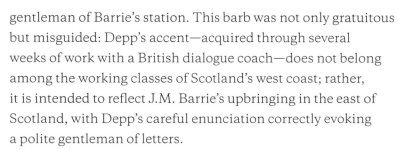

Above: Tea and sympathy for the ailing Sylvia Llewelyn Davies (Kate Winslet).

Right: Reality shifts into fantasy as Barrie and the Llewelyn Davies family act out *Peter Pan*.

gentleman of Barrie's station. This barb was not only gratuitous but misguided: Depp's accent—acquired through several weeks of work with a British dialogue coach—does not belong among the working classes of Scotland's west coast; rather, it is intended to reflect J.M. Barrie's upbringing in the east of Scotland, with Depp's careful enunciation correctly evoking a polite gentleman of letters.

Overall, the reviews for *Finding Neverland* were fairly lukewarm, with many critics complaining that it was a drama that came to life only when it was too late. There was no shortage of reviewers who enumerated various biographical facts that Magee had excised from the original stage play; but such criticism is never to be taken too seriously, since it has been applied to virtually every biopic ever made. (And, yes, J.M. Barrie did indeed sport a moustache in addition to being considerably less handsome than, and seven inches shorter than, Johnny Depp.) Another set of British reviewers remembered a three-part TV mini-series entitled *The Lost Boys*, which the BBC

had broadcast in 1978; it was hardly surprising that they declared this nuanced four-and-a-half-hour drama to be superior to Marc Forster's film, which clocked in at a modest 106 minutes.

Johnny Depp is a revelation in *Finding Neverland*, handing in one of the most finely calibrated performances of his career. Writing in the *New Yorker*, Anthony Lane found the actor to be "charmingly innocent of guile," a phrase which could quite possibly be applied to most of Depp's oeuvre. In *Finding Neverland*, J.M. Barrie effortlessly interacts with, and becomes fascinated by, the Llewelyn Davies children, whom he addresses more or less as equals. The boys reciprocate Barrie's respect, with the notable exception of the third son, Peter (played by the precocious Freddie Highmore), who keeps a wary distance from this whimsical adult interloper.

As Barrie's relationship with the family grows stronger, it brings about the end of his moribund marriage and draws disapproving comment from Mrs. Llewelyn Davies' mother (sardonically played by the venerable Julie Christie).

None of this gives Barrie any sleepless nights, because he sees his interplay coalescing into the theme for his new play, about Peter Pan, a boyish character who simply refuses to grow up.

*Peter Pan* also has darker origins within the more distant recesses of Barrie's psyche: When he was just six years old, his 13-year-old brother, David, died in an ice-skating accident. Their mother was left entirely inconsolable, and the younger son spent years fruitlessly attempting to rekindle the spark in her eyes. All these years later, Barrie has still not dealt with the emotional damage wrought upon him by David's death; but by creating the perpetually youthful character of Peter Pan, he gives himself the chance to address, albeit indirectly, his unresolved feelings about the loss of his beloved brother.

By the time *Peter Pan* finally takes shape, it is clear that Kate Winslet's character is far too ill to attend the play's opening night—so Barrie arranges for a truncated performance in the Davies house. At this point the film is as unstoppable as our impulse to reach out for the nearest Kleenex.

Despite the doubts of Barrie's agent, *Peter Pan* opens in late December 1904. There's an old adage that "there's no sight so impressive as a Scotsman on the make," and the playwright reveals his pragmatic side by placing a group of two-dozen orphans right in the middle of the opening-night audience. Yes, it's Kleenex time again. *Peter Pan* is a roaring success, and the rest, as they say, is black ink on the Disney company's balance sheet.

*Finding Neverland* received seven Oscar nominations, including one for Depp, but as it transpired only composer Jan Kaczmarek walked away with a little gold statue. For Depp it was enough that the $25 million film had made more than $115 million worldwide; his new status as a global superstar had been enhanced by the unusual experience of scoring two hit movies in quick succession. However, anyone who imagined that Hollywood's most quixotic celebrity was spending any time planning a third major hit would probably be well advised to lay off the pixie dust.

"*The film never seems to go quite where you expect it to go. It never turns into a sentimental love story of two people destined to be together or that sort of thing.*"

Opposite: Johnny Depp as Scottish playwright J.M. Barrie in *Finding Neverland*.

Left: The Miramax publicity machine working flat out for *Finding Neverland*. Front cover of *Life*, November 2004.

Above: At the Screen Actors Guild Awards, February 2005, with co-star Freddie Highmore and partner Vanessa Paradis.

# The Libertine

2004
·················

"I felt this very
strong responsibility
to play him right—
so much so that I
became obsessed.
I read everything.
I knew everything
about him."

Johnny Depp

The Libertine

*"I always felt he was this great, great poet who was never acknowledged as a great poet, but looked upon as a satirist or some silly guy who hung around the court of King Charles II. I never believed he got his due. He was a renegade, a brilliant poet who was incredibly brave."*

Contrasting scenes with Rosamund Pike as Elizabeth Malet.

On paper *The Libertine* looked like a perfect fit for Johnny Depp, brought about by a perfect confluence of events. The movie is an adaptation of Stephen Jeffreys' successful stage play, which debuted in London in late 1994, and made its US bow at Chicago's Steppenwolf Theater in early 1996. During that initial Chicago run, *The Libertine*'s main character, John Wilmot, second Earl of Rochester, was played by John Malkovich, who brought Johnny Depp to see the play in the hopes that he would agree to star in a film version.

Eight years later, when Malkovich's plans to film *The Libertine* were finally coming to fruition, Depp jumped at the chance to participate. The knowledge that he could bank on lucrative sequels of *Pirates of the Caribbean: The Curse of the Black Pearl* had brought Depp an unprecedented measure of financial security, and Rochester was exactly the kind of character he wanted to play. The Earl was a notorious seventeenth-century peer who lived fast and died young in 1680; he was one of England's most notorious hedonists, who had a sideline in writing poetry that was well regarded in respectable circles despite being scandalously ribald by the standard of the times. (The vast majority of Rochester's poems went unpublished during his lifetime; after they eventually saw the light of day their author found favor with such literary giants as Johann Wolfgang von Goethe, who quoted him; and Voltaire, who called him a "genius.")

In the words of Samuel Johnson, Rochester's was "a life spent in ostentatious contempt of regularity" before he "blazed out his youth and health in lavish voluptuousness." In late 2005, Depp told London's *Evening Standard* why he felt an affinity for this world-class roué upon reading his story. "I recognized something that I had gone through," Depp said. "I quit drinking spirits because I wouldn't stop. I would just keep going until a black screen came down where you can't see anything any more and you don't know if you're around."

The big-screen iteration of *The Libertine* would see John Malkovich assuming the secondary role of Charles II and Depp taking center stage as the 30-ish John Wilmot. Screenplay duties would be handled by the play's original writer Stephen Jeffreys. *The Libertine* began shooting in England and Wales in early 2004, only to be abruptly derailed when the British government closed the tax loophole that made the whole production financially viable. In his capacity as producer, Malkovich hastily reconfigured the movie's production schedule to incorporate the less fiscally stringent Isle of Man as a new location. Meanwhile the break in filming allowed Johnny Depp to pore over the cache of Rochester research material that's housed at London's British Museum; this only served further to heighten his affinity for the character he was playing.

The film takes place over the last few years of Rochester's life, culminating in his death, at the age of 33, from syphilis. During this period Rochester maintained an uneasy place within the court of King Charles II; the story begins with the King summoning his dissipated subject back to London shortly after expelling him for a year for his insolent behavior. Upon his return to the capital, Rochester happens upon a struggling actress named Elizabeth Barry (Samantha Morton), whom he quickly coaches to greatness using a method not unlike *the* Method, as pioneered by Lee Strasberg in the mid-twentieth century. His response to her refusal of carnality is to rejoin his mates on their never-ending round of boozing and whoring.

When the shifty-eyed King Charles commissions Rochester to write a play for the visiting French ambassador, whom the King wants to impress for financial reasons, what he gets is a smorgasbord of graphic smut presented in homage to the dildo. Rochester himself is performing this piece of filth when the King gets up on stage to halt the proceeding; the errant playwright flees to his country estate, where a severe dose of syphilis grotesquely transfigures his appearance before ultimately killing him.

> *"I perused his actual letters in the British Library and found his words and made notes and used them in the script. Without wanting to sound all kind of New Agey, I do believe that he paid me at least a few visits."*

Opposite: Being interviewed at the Los Angeles premiere of *The Libertine*, November 2005. The movie was not released across the US until March 2006.

The hedonistic Earl of Rochester, a role originally played on stage in the mid-nineties by John Malkovich.

For several reasons, both palpable and intangible, *The Libertine* never comes close to fulfilling the abundant promise it appeared to have before the cameras started rolling. Among the more obvious flaws in the piece is that, although the glamorously accoutered Rochester boasts incessantly of his sexual prowess, director Laurence Dunmore (a music-video veteran who did not make another film after *The Libertine*) does not feel obliged to back up his protagonist's words with action. There is hardly a single moment of the movie that one could categorize as "erotic," and Rochester's hints at bisexual proclivities go unexamined.

Plus, for all its upper-middlebrow credentials and dense verbosity, *The Libertine* offers precious little in terms of memorable dialogue. Strange as it may sound, the first *Pirates of the Caribbean* film contains more pithy morsels of antiquated English than Jeffreys' esteemed drama.

Of the actors involved in this misfiring project, only Samantha Morton emerges with any real credit. John Malkovich is as watchable as ever, but the role of Charles II gives him little opportunity to unleash the saturnine smirk and general air of moral corruption that brought him such good notices when he played Rochester in Chicago eight years earlier. Which means that some of the blame for *The Libertine*'s shortcomings must be placed at the elegantly shod feet of Johnny Depp; because, while he has certainly had his own periods of overindulgence, his desire to channel them into the Rochester character was ultimately misguided. Paradoxically, it may have been to Depp's advantage that the belated release of *The Libertine* was such a low-key, staggered affair (it was first shown at the Toronto Film Festival in September 2004, but did not receive a general release in the US until March 2006)—the film's predominantly negative reviews were drowned out by all the attention paid to the more successful Depp movies of this time, the family-friendly *Charlie and the Chocolate Factory*, *Corpse Bride*, and *Finding Neverland*.

# Charlie and the Chocolate Factory

2005

....................

"To be chosen to play Willy Wonka in itself is a great honor, but to be chosen by Tim Burton is double, triple the honor."

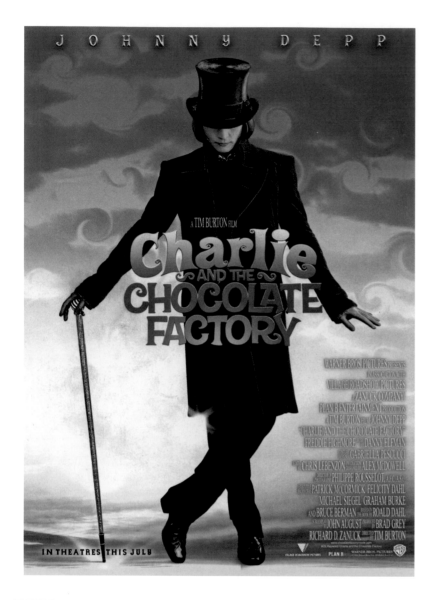

The phenomenal commercial success of Tim Burton's ham-fisted 2001 *Planet of the Apes* re-make may have silenced some of the film's many critics, but there were still enough disciples of the original 1968 version to make the director's life uncomfortable. As Burton subsequently noted about his *Planet of the Apes* experience, "I knew I was walking into an ambush."

Yet here was Tim Burton, four years later, re-making another beloved movie from the same pop-cultural epoch as *Planet of the Apes*. It was almost as though the creator of *Edward Scissorhands* and *Sleepy Hollow* had fallen into the fervid grip of some condition that compelled him to re-work formative movies of his childhood. Fortunately for Burton, the 1971 kids' film *Willy Wonka & the Chocolate Factory* did not set the bar nearly as high as had *Planet of the Apes*, so revisiting it—under the title of Roald Dahl's original book, *Charlie and the Chocolate Factory*—should not have presented too many problems.

Burton had been able to overcome the largest obstacle to making the film, which was the family of the late Roald Dahl (the writer died in 1990). Dahl reputedly hated the 1971 *Willy Wonka* film: Although Dahl himself had written the screenplay, director Mel Stuart commissioned additional material without the author's approval, and generally failed to convey the misanthropic tone of the original story. During subsequent decades there were rumors about various major-league directors and stars who wanted to take a shot at a re-make, but the source material was made inaccessible to them.

In 1991 Tim Burton, with the backing of Warner Bros. Pictures, approached the Dahl family about the idea of filming a new movie version of *Charlie and the Chocolate Factory*, but the family did not reach an agreement with Warner until 1998. It wasn't until 2003 that Burton turned his attention back to the Dahl project, which would be financed partly by Plan B Productions, a company formed by Brad Pitt and Jennifer

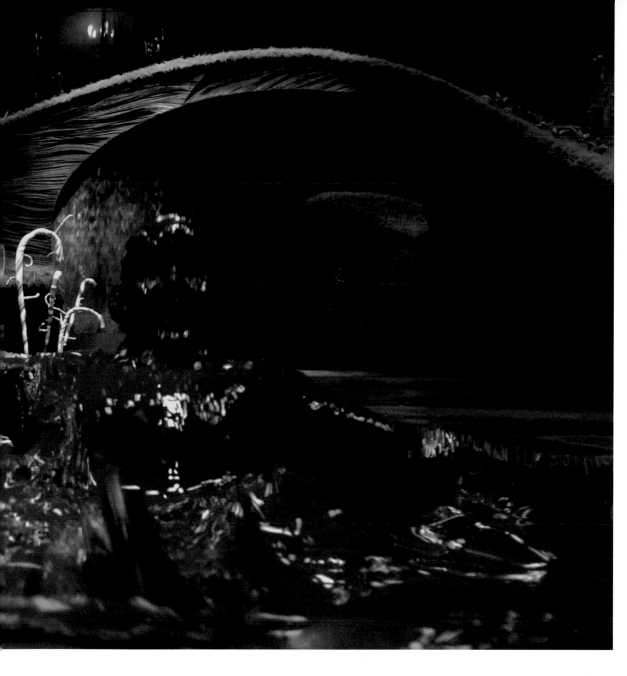

*"Early on, the hardest part was trying to erase any memory I had of the 1971 film with Gene Wilder. And then you go, 'Christ, I can't erase it, so I'll just have to make a very, very sharp left turn.'"*

The gluttonous Augustus Gloop (Philip Wiegratz) gets his comeuppance in Willy Wonka's chocolate lake.

Aniston during their short-lived marriage. When Burton asked Johnny Depp if he'd consider playing the lead role of Willy Wonka, Depp's response was immediate and positive.

The prospect of Tim Burton and Johnny Depp making *Charlie and the Chocolate Factory* did not appeal to everyone: The most prominent dissenter was Gene Wilder, star of the original film, who issued a public statement on the whole affair as the new movie was going into production. "It's all about money," asserted Wilder. "Why else would you re-make *Willy Wonka*?" Depp later acknowledged that since Wilder's performance was "definitive and [was] seared into everyone's brains," creating a new *Willy Wonka* presented him with a not-insubstantial challenge.

Although Gene Wilder later spoke out in support of Burton and Depp's venture, the director didn't hesitate to emphasize that he had never harbored any intentions of "re-making" *Willy Wonka*; his prime objective was to create a film that reflected

Roald Dahl's original vision, something which clearly hadn't troubled the creators of the 1971 movie. "I don't want to crush people's original dreams," said Burton of his twenty-first-century *Chocolate Factory*. "But the original film is sappy. It's sappy when it shouldn't be sappy, and it's weird."

Few would dispute that Roald Dahl's *Charlie and the Chocolate Factory* is among the weirdest books ever to be designated a "children's classic." Dahl's story depicts a contest in which a handful of Golden Tickets are hidden in chocolate bars made by the oddball confectionery mogul Willy Wonka. The kids who find said items are taken on a tour of Wonka's manufacturing plant, a dark, satanic edifice with an interior that one might describe as "psychedelic" had the original book been published slightly later than 1964.

Dahl's tale takes a turn for the allegorical as four of Willy Wonka's young guests disappear, one by one. The lone survivor is Charlie Bucket (played by Depp's *Finding Neverland* co-star

*"I tried to interpret what Roald Dahl created in the book—the twisted, perverted side of the character. I had in mind children's TV presenters from when I was a kid."*

Freddie Highmore), the only member of the tour group who isn't spoiled or brattish in some way. In a 2005 interview with French film historian Antoine de Baecque, Burton—who had, two years earlier, had a son with English actress Helena Bonham Carter—sounded unusually serious when explaining why he saw the new *Chocolate Factory* film as a cautionary tale of sorts.

"I don't like what our society does to children," stated Burton. "We constantly subject them to all these jostling, competing things. It's both an abdication of responsibility and a form of cynicism, a way of spoiling them and enjoying a peaceful life." Just to drive home the point, Burton's film shows the Bucket family living amid a virtual parody of Dickensian poverty. (Helena Bonham Carter, whom Burton has cast in all of his movies from *Planet of the Apes* onwards, portrayed Charlie's mother.)

Like *Willy Wonka* director, Mel Stuart, Tim Burton seemed to have felt that the original *Chocolate Factory* story was lacking in narrative heft, because he too commissioned new material

for his film. In Burton's movie the supplemental scenes are designed to explain how the extraordinary Mr. Wonka came to be the way he is. Burton decided that veteran English horror-movie star Christopher Lee (another actor who'd be given roles in several other Burton films) was the perfect fit for the part of Wonka's tyrannical dentist father, who bans his boy from eating candy and ultimately causes him to flee the family home.

Burton's 2005 interview with Antoine de Baecque saw him reveal, with unusual directness, the inspiration behind the new material. "I have to admit, young Willy Wonka is me," said Burton. "I had huge teeth and I wore a brace that I hated... This guy is an embodiment of what happened to me as a small boy."

Johnny Depp does not have his first full scene as Willy Wonka until the film is over half an hour old, at which point we start to get a proper sense of how he's responded to the Wonka challenge. All that Depp's Wonka has in common with Gene Wilder's version of the character is a top hat: Wilder played the

Opposite: Johnny Depp and Tim Burton share their concept of Willy Wonka.

Right: Willy Wonka shows off Wonkavision to Mike Teavee (Jordan Fry), his dad (Adam Godley), Charlie Bucket (Freddie Highmore), and Charlie's grandpa Joe (David Kelly). For television-obsessed Mike Teavee, the temptation to get on the other side of the screen is too great.

part on the verge of comedic hysteria, as was his habit, whereas Depp is ice-cool, lending Wonka a sheen of artifice. Both Depp and Burton have mentioned reclusive millionaire Howard Hughes as one psychological reference point for their reading of Willy Wonka, a perma-gloved "germophobe" who sports oversized perfect teeth and outdated Prince Valiant-style bangs.

Depp and Burton imbued this new Willy Wonka with a trait that many audience members may well have missed at first glance: Partly inspired by some of the incongruous kids' TV hosts of their respective childhoods, the two men decided to show Wonka periodically sneaking a peek at his "lines" on cue-cards. Although Tim Burton eschews the use of CGI effects in his fourth Johnny Depp collaboration in 15 years, *Charlie and the Chocolate Factory* is a crisp, brightly lit, and somehow demystified affair. While its $150 million budget is visibly manifested in Burton's succession of inventive tableaux vivants—such as a 200,000-gallon "river" made of liquid "chocolate," with attendant "waterfall"—the film never manages to cast as powerful a spell as did its low-tech, fuzzy-looking precursor. Furthermore, for a putative comedy... there aren't really any genuine laughs. In the end the difference between Burton's film and *Willy Wonka*, between Depp's characterization and Gene Wilder's, is as pronounced as the gulf between analogue and digital.

*Time* magazine's Richard Schickel offered a concise take on one widespread criticism of Burton and Depp's latest endeavor. "There's a distance, a detachment to this film," Schickel wrote. "It lacks passion." Even the movie's supporters did not seem entirely convinced of its merits.

Still, as with *Planet of the Apes*, Burton had created a film to which the public flocked in large numbers, in spite of largely mixed-to-negative reviews. *Charlie and the Chocolate Factory* eventually grossed $475 million worldwide, although—like Burton's *Planet of the Apes*—neither the film's imagery nor its performances remained in the mass consciousness for very long.

# Pirates of the Caribbean

## Dead Man's Chest
2006
..................

## At World's End
2007
..................

"I miss Captain Jack.
I'm looking forward to
meeting him again."

*"It was almost like a crime to have so much fun."*

Left: Movie mogul Jerry Bruckheimer (center) gets in on the joke with director Gore Verbinski and Johnny Depp.

Below: The second *Pirates* movie opened in more than 50 countries. Here, the poster for the Russian release.

Opposite: Captain Jack leaves the hard work to Ragetti (Mackenzie Crook), Pintel (Lee Arenberg), Will Turner (Orlando Bloom, hidden), and Norrington (Jack Davenport) before retreating to the comfort of his trailer.

ПИРАТЫ КАРИБСКОГО МОРЯ
ПРОКЛЯТЬЕ ЧЕРНОЙ ЖЕМЧУЖИНЫ

**A**fter the barnstorming success of *Pirates of the Caribbean: The Curse of the Black Pearl*, Walt Disney Pictures decided to follow a precedent set by Warner Bros. when the first of its *Matrix* movies became a money-spinning sleeper hit in 1999, and order up two sequels to be filmed together. While such a strategy doubtless makes a great deal of sense to corporate accounting departments, the second and third installments of the *Pirates* series prove how much of a strain it can put on the creative talent behind a global movie franchise.

Both *Dead Man's Chest* and *At World's End* saw Disney retaining the services of director Gore Verbinski and writers Ted Elliott and Terry Rossio. On paper, at least, these three men didn't look like a team that would turn a movie based on a theme-park ride into one of the biggest earners of all time.

Remember that Verbinski's last job pre-*Pirates* had been a 2002 US re-make of the Japanese horror flick *The Ring*; and while Elliott and Rossio had proved their mettle with *Aladdin* (1992) and *Shrek* (2001), not even Disney could have expected the pair to come up with anything as lucrative as Captain Jack Sparrow, the character who indisputably made the movie viable

Consumer culture: Fleeing cannibal tribesmen who intend to express their worship of Captain Jack by eating him.

as a franchise. And not only was Johnny Depp a most unlikely front man for the whole escapade, Disney executives had made extremely discouraging noises when they first glimpsed his pirate-as-rock-star routine on the set of *Black Pearl*.

Yet here they all were in April 2005, resuming the *Pirates* enterprise on a grander scale, having earned back more than four times the $140 million budget of the first film. Major movie studios do not tend to make public the precise details of what they spend on individual films, and there was the added complication of *Dead Man's Chest* being filmed back to back with *At World's End*; but it is generally agreed that when the whole operation lumbered into action, *Dead Man's Chest* was slated to cost Disney somewhere in the region of $220 million. In that context Depp's reported $20 million-per-movie salary for the first three *Pirates* outings seemed like a pretty good deal for his paymasters.

It's clear from the outset that the creators of *Pirates of the Caribbean: Dead Man's Chest* are making a Herculean effort to top their first film—and therein lies the problem. *Curse*

*of the Black Pearl* was a happy accident, a giddy pop-culture phenomenon that owed much of its success to Johnny Depp's singular interpretation of Captain Jack Sparrow. The audience that came in such numbers to see that movie had done so because of the seemingly effortless way in which Depp brought the Captain to life; generally speaking, people do not go to the cinema to see men at work.

In *Dead Man's Chest* Ted Elliott and Terry Rossio's laboriously constructed plot involves the conflation of maritime legends like Davy Jones' Locker, the *Flying Dutchman*, and the kraken, alongside exaggerated versions of historical events—a version of the Dutch East India Company is featured, to foreshadow the multinational corporations of coming centuries. The most notable addition to the cast is the revered English character actor Bill Nighy, who is augmented by both prosthetic makeup and CGI effects to play tentacle-faced bad guy Davy Jones, to whom Captain Jack owes a "blood debt." Swedish actor Stellan Skarsgård plays Bootstrap Bill Turner, the father of

Sparrow's sidekick Will Turner (Orlando Bloom), who returns to the series along with his beloved, the plucky Elizabeth Swann (Keira Knightley).

In a textbook display of kitchen-sink filmmaking Gore Verbinski uses every weapon in his $220 million arsenal to ensure that the pace of *Dead Man's Chest* never slackens. However, in doing so the director creates a bombastic sound-and-light show that only adds to the confusion created by the movie's convoluted plot. Paradoxically, the dialogue for *Dead Man's Chest* sparkles as brightly as ever, and pearls of roguish philosophy tumble forth from Captain Jack's lips throughout.

Few movie actors get the opportunity to expand on a character over the course of multiple films, and Johnny Depp does not abuse the privilege, developing Jack Sparrow into an ever-more captivating figure. Members of the press are always keen to play up Depp's self-confessed debt to Keith Richards (who failed to make a planned appearance in *Dead Man's Chest*) for inspiring his characterization of Sparrow, but the

actor actually owes considerably more to another English star of the rock era, David Bowie. While there is a touch of Richards' debauched country gent about Depp's performance, the camp whimsy of 1970s Bowie is far more evident as Jack Sparrow trips the light fantastic from one misadventure to another. In terms of movie archetypes, Depp uses Jack Sparrow to reinvent the charming but cowardly rogue as personified by Bob Hope and W.C. Fields before him.

If nothing else the job of deconstructing Captain Jack tended to bring out the best in movie critics: *Rolling Stone*'s Peter Travers, for instance, called Depp's creation a "bisexual narcissist with a devilish glint that suggests he'll never tell you where he stashed his drug kit." Unfortunately this kind of goodwill was not extended to the film in general; there was a groundswell of disapproval, as evidenced by headlines like "Johnny Depp Shakes His Booty But *Pirates of the Caribbean* Is Just a Rum Joke." Those were the words that appeared above a *Washington Post* review which declared that this "encore

Captain Jack enjoys the veneration of the headhunters not knowing yet what they have in store for him (top); contests a three-way sword fight with Norrington and Turner (bottom); and takes his crew to the shack of voodoo priestess Tia Dalma (opposite).

*"When we started out on Pirates 1, it was very simple, like any other character: You just sort of grab bits and pieces and out comes this kind of weird little stew you've created. And then, boom! It's the first time I was ever offered the opportunity to find a couple more possibilities. It's just so much fun to get away with things you're not normally allowed to do. He's totally irreverent, played as absurd as you like."*

Right: The wardrobe department gets to work on Barbossa (Geoffrey Rush), Elizabeth Swann (Keira Knightley), and Captain Jack Sparrow.

feels forced and hollow—a repeat performance that's too self-consciously delivered to be charming anymore."

As always, such matters are in the eye of the beholder, and the commercial performance of *Dead Man's Chest* suggested that a significant number of people were charmed by the way in which Depp shook his booty. The movie swiftly entered the exalted cluster of films that have earned over $1 billion.

Before *Pirates of the Caribbean: At World's End* was shot, the crew had to rebuild a set that was destroyed by a hurricane during the filming of *Dead Man's Chest*. Something else that was lost in the process of making the second *Pirates* movie was apparently its creators' sense of self-restraint, because the third

part of the Captain Jack Sparrow saga is even more bombastic than its predecessor.

Once again, the manner of its production makes it harder than usual to discern exact figures, but the budget for *At World's End* has been estimated at somewhere around $300 million, which would make it the most expensive film ever made. As with *Dead Man's Chest*, the final product is grandiose in scale; and once again, that proves no guarantee of a watchable picture.

Captain Jack Sparrow does not appear on the screen until over half an hour of the film has passed; although when he does materialize it's in the mind-bending form of multiple computer-generated images. As any filmgoer would instantly recognize,

this has to be a dream—and when Captain Jack wakes up he finds himself in yet another tight spot.

There are times when this mind-boggling 169-minute behemoth seems to channel the spirit of a triple concept album by some 1970s pomp-rock outfit—which is mildly ironic given the punk-rock affiliation shared by Johnny Depp and director Gore Verbinski. By *At World's End* the *Pirates* series had developed its own, elaborate internal logic, creating a hermetic universe that would make your head spin if you paused to think about it for too long.

Keith Richards finally shows up, making a cameo as Jack Sparrow's long-lost father Captain Teague, but he's too late to rescue the picture. Geoffrey Rush is dependably droll as Captain

Like a Rolling Stone? The often-observed debt Captain Jack owes to Keith Richards is repaid in *At World's End* with a cameo role for the veteran rocker. Richards plays Jack's father Captain Teague.

Overleaf: Portrait by Matt Sayles, Beverly Hills, June 2006.

Jack's recurring rival Hector Barbossa, and Keira Knightley's terminally sincere Elizabeth Swann provides a nice foil for Sparrow and his improvised morality. However, Swann and her beau, Will Turner, are so insubstantial that by this point in the series they have turned into ciphers for "star-crossed lovers"; fortunately for everyone involved, the writers neatly tie up their storyline at the movie's end.

In the lull between the second and third episodes, Rush had joked that, at the climax of *Dead Man's Chest*, "12 plots all converge on one massive, almost mythological, action sequence," but he was not too far from the mark. In fact, Johnny Depp more or less admitted as much in an *Entertainment Weekly* interview several years after the fact. "It was plot-driven and complicated," Depp allowed.

Before the *Pirates* phenomenon took off, Depp was always at pains to express his discomfort with the whole notion of celebrity, and consciously set himself apart from the expectations that a movie star is usually obliged to fulfill. But a few years after *The Curse of the Black Pearl* it seemed that Depp had

reached an understanding with franchise-driven fame by applying a peculiar, slightly convoluted rationale to the whole process. In the run-up to the release of *Dead Man's Chest*, he told *Entertainment Weekly*, "It's fascinating to witness the machine at work, watch it hum and scream and howl. To see these products, like cereal boxes and fruit chews and action figures and sheets and towels and pillows... I mean, we've entered the arena where Marcel Duchamp and Andy Warhol are Snoopy-dancing in the nude. It's so absurd and so surreal and so irreverent that I love it."

The release of *At World's End* brought out the worst in movie reviewers: No pirate analogy was left behind as they laid into this overcooked spectacle. Some even suspended Depp's normal exemption from criticism. However, when the film was released the appeal of watching Johnny Depp cavorting around in eyeliner, with a hip quip forever on his lip, proved irresistible, and receipts fell only slightly short of the $1 billion earned by *Dead Man's Chest*. As they say in Tinseltown, "No one liked it but the public."

"Captain Jack has
brought a lot of good
things into my world,
and into my kiddies'
world. I'll always hold
him in very high regard.
It's been an absolute
pleasure to play him;
frankly, it's been a
total blast."

I've been around long enough to know that one week, you're on the exclusive list of guys who can open a movie, and then the next week, you're off the list. It's been a fun ride, and I'm enjoying it for all it's worth."

# Sweeney Todd

## The Demon Barber
## of Fleet Street

2007

"I'm a big fan of
revenge!"

This $50 million movie adaptation of Stephen Sondheim's Tony-winning musical prompted Tim Burton to divulge a dirty little secret about himself: When he was visiting London during his days as a CalArts animation student, Burton stumbled across a production of *Sweeney Todd*—and was so mesmerized by it that he came back to see the show on several successive evenings. Just in case his followers got the wrong idea, Burton added the caveat, "I liked [movie musical] *Cat Ballou*. I liked *Guys and Dolls*. But I'm not on Broadway every night or sitting at home watching *Sound of Music*."

Sondheim's *Sweeney Todd: The Demon Barber of Fleet Street* opened on March 1, 1979 at the Uris Theater (now the Gershwin Theater) on 51st Street in New York's theater district, picking up eight Tony Awards (including one for Best Score) early in its 557-performance run. The musical—with "book" written by Hugh Wheeler—was based on a 1973 stage play about the mythical London murderer, who first appeared in Thomas Peckett Prest's 1846 story *The String of Pearls: A Romance*, which was serialized by the "penny dreadful" weekly *The People's*

*Periodical*. This ghoulish figure turned out to be surprisingly durable, and was reincarnated in numerous stage, film, and media adaptations during the twentieth century.

Persuading Stephen Sondheim to allow his musical to be adapted for the big screen was probably even more of a coup for Burton than his earlier acquisition of the movie rights for Roald Dahl's *Charlie and the Chocolate Factory*, because a virtual Who's Who of Hollywood stars and directors had attempted to gain Sondheim's approval for a *Sweeney Todd* movie since the show first appeared on Broadway.

Although Burton and Sondheim may look like the most unlikely of bedfellows—the San Fernando Valley goth and the New York haut aesthete—they first discussed a *Sweeney Todd* adaptation in the 1990s. Sondheim (the composer and lyricist behind such money-spinning shows as *Company*, *Follies*, and *A Little Night Music*) had been dissatisfied with previous movies derived from his work, but was apparently happy to entrust his 1979 brainchild to the director of *Beetlejuice* and *Mars Attacks!* However, the composer had serious reservations about Burton's

Opposite: Tim Burton had long hoped to make a movie adaptation of Stephen Sondheim's acclaimed musical. The result delighted critics, audiences, and Sondheim alike.

Right: With goatee back in place, Johnny Depp arrives at a special screening of *Sweeney Todd*, Paramount Studios, Hollywood, December 2007.

JOHNNY DEPP
IS
SWEENEY TODD
THE DEM  ER OF FLEET STREET
THIS CHRISTMAS

wish to cast Johnny Depp in the title role, believing that the actor's voice would be too "rock-oriented" for a Broadway-born musical. This placed Burton in the now-unfamiliar position of having to defend his decision to cast Depp in a movie; fortunately Depp had, as always, been most diligent in his preparation, and his musical audition tape allayed Sondheim's fears.

"Sweeney Todd" is the pseudonym adopted by a London barber named Benjamin Barker who, at the start of Sondheim's musical, has just returned from 17 years' penal servitude. Barker was exiled by the corrupt and venal Judge Turpin, who then kidnapped his wife and daughter, raping the former and inducing her suicide. As Sweeney Todd, Barker is intent on having his revenge on Turpin, and finds the optimum accomplice in Mrs. Nellie Lovett, proprietor of a struggling London meat-pie emporium.

Mrs. Lovett conceals her infatuation with Sweeney Todd, even as she reunites him with the glistening tools of his trade. He sets about killing an impressive number of citizens with his open razor, and disposes of the bodies with the aid of a mechanized barber's chair that dumps them beneath the floorboards of his shop. Lovett aids Todd in a manner that defines the whole tale: by grinding up the corpses, baking them in pies, and selling them to an eager public.

Tim Burton's cinematic *Sweeney Todd* sees Johnny Depp plucking a new arrow from his artistic quiver. While Sweeney Todd firmly belongs to Depp's collection of neurotic outsider characters, there is nothing boyish about this homicidal

hairdresser. Depp's Todd has flowing black locks that are distinguished by the gray streak that runs back from his right temple. The face underneath is gaunt and haunted, and about as far from *21 Jump Street* as it's possible to get.

The plot of *Sweeney Todd* may be melodramatic in the extreme, but Depp is a model of low-key restraint during every second of his screen time. Like Burton (and indeed Sondheim), the actor fully appreciated the vast difference in the demands imposed by a theatrical piece and a feature film. Among Depp's many able supporting colleagues, Helena Bonham Carter, as Mrs. Lovett, should be singled out for special mention: This was an actress who was already extremely accomplished before she became romantically involved with Tim Burton, but had been frequently taken for granted since she began appearing in his films—among other things, *Sweeney Todd* served to remind the world of Bonham Carter's worth.

When the *Sweeney Todd* movie was announced, *Variety* assumed that Tim Burton would be taking what it termed an "unprofesh" approach to Stephen Sondheim's material with

Depp and Bonham Carter on board, and wondered how this might go down with hard-core Sondheimites. The magazine's concerns were misplaced, because the director was both reverential and thorough in his execution, offering a grim and highly distinctive vision of London during its peak years as the soot-encrusted fulcrum of the industrial age.

Johnny Depp had never sung an entire song by himself on film before appearing as Sweeney Todd, so it is a tribute to his dauntless application that he was able to handle so confidently the lead role in a musical. Depp may not quite be ready to join the list of celebrity audience-pleasers who have been strutting their stuff in Broadway shows over the last decade or so, but he has a fairly tolerable tenor, and copes well with Sondheim's sometimes mathematically complex songs. Some British critics, unlike most of their US counterparts, noticed a distinct resemblance between Depp's singing voice and that of David Bowie during his early, Anthony Newley-inspired phase. This seemingly obvious musical homage further highlighted the similarities between Bowie and Depp's iconic *Pirates of the Caribbean* character

*"I knew I wouldn't be tone deaf but I wasn't sure I could carry a song, let alone several, and something as complex as Stephen Sondheim's. It was real scary for both of us. And talk about the opportunity to really flop."*

"At last! My arm is complete again!" Reunited with his trusty razor, and in league with Mrs. Lovett (Helena Bonham Carter), the demon barber guarantees his customers "the closest shave they'll ever know."

Overleaf: Attending the UK premiere of *Sweeney Todd*, London, January 2008.

Captain Jack Sparrow—yet once again critics completely missed the connection, preferring to emphasize Sparrow's less-marked resemblance to Keith Richards.

Tim Burton's corporate partner in making *Sweeney Todd* was Warner Bros., and when the company's executives saw the initial version of the film they asked the director to make a significant reduction in its violent content in order that the film qualify for an accessible "R" rating. Burton reluctantly complied, so we may never know what sanguinary heights were originally reached by a film that still ends with what is surely one of the Grandest Guignols ever seen in a mainstream production.

When Warner scheduled the release of *Sweeney Todd: The Demon Barber of Fleet Street* for just before Christmas 2007, there were those who questioned the wisdom of unleashing such a bloodthirsty beast in the middle of what has traditionally been family season at the box office. However, the timing proved to be a brilliant stroke of counterintuitive marketing: *Sweeney Todd* was a major hit before 2008 dawned, and the film went on to bring in over $150 million internationally. Depp's portrayal of

the demon barber brought him a Golden Globe Award (Helena Bonham Carter and Tim Burton were also nominated) and an Oscar nomination—although in the end production designer Dante Ferretti and set decorator Francesca Lo Schiavo won the movie's sole Academy Award, for Art Direction.

This was not one of the many Tim Burton projects that critics have greeted with studied ambivalence. Reviews were among the most positive he'd seen for years, and the film won over some of the major-league critics who'd always harbored reservations about Burton. *Newsweek*'s David Ansen, for instance, said that the director's "strength has never been storytelling—his Gothic imagination flowers episodically—but *Sweeney Todd*, his best movie since *Ed Wood*... has the relentless forward momentum of a shark in blood-stained waters."

Tim Burton had to wait a couple more years for probably the only review that mattered to him personally. In Stephen Sondheim's 2010 book *Finishing the Hat,* the composer declared that *Sweeney Todd* was the only one of his works that had "found a satisfactory cinematic transposition."

I've never felt particularly ambitious or driven, that's for sure, although I like to create stuff, whether it's a little doodle, a drawing, a small painting or a movie or a piece of music, so I suppose I'm driven by that."

SAMUEL HADIDA présente

un film de **TERRY GILLIAM**

**JOHNNY DEPP**
est **Tony, l'envoûteur**.
*Découvrez son monde de magie.*

FESTIVAL DE CANNES
SÉLECTION OFFICIELLE

# L'IMAGINARIUM DU DOCTEUR PARNASSUS

docteurparnassus.com   **AU CINÉMA LE 11 NOVEMBRE**   INFINITY FEATURES   Canada   MANDATE INTERNATIONAL   DAVIS

METROPOLITAN FILMEXPORT

# The Imaginarium of Doctor Parnassus

2009

"It was an awful, awful time. It was just hard to believe… confusing. But all that mattered was saving the work that Heath had done."

Above: Heath Ledger, the original Tony, here with Doctor Parnassus's daughter Valentina (Lily Cole). Ledger died suddenly a third of the way through filming and his role was performed by three leading actors, including Johnny Depp.

Previous page: The poster for the film's French release.

W hile Johnny Depp's contribution to this film constitutes little more than a cameo, the circumstances of its creation lend it a great significance within the broader context of Depp's personal biography.

*Doctor Parnassus* was directed and co-written by Terry Gilliam, the mercurial auteur with whom Depp had worked in 1998 on *Fear and Loathing in Las Vegas*. The film began shooting in December 2007, with Christopher Plummer as the superannuated showman Doctor Parnassus; playing his latest sidekick, a young trickster known simply as Tony, was Heath Ledger, the 28-year-old Australian whose performance in *Brokeback Mountain* (2005) had earned him an Oscar nomination, along with widespread expectations of bigger things to come. On January 22, 2008, during a scheduled break in production, Ledger was spending some time alone in his New York apartment when he fatally overdosed on a combination of prescription drugs.

Once the initial wave of shock and grief had subsided, Terry Gilliam initially resigned himself to the idea that *Doctor Parnassus* would, like his feature *The Man Who Killed Don Quixote*

(started in 2000), never be completed. However, it occurred to Gilliam that the current film's plot could potentially contain the solution to what initially seemed like an intractable problem.

Doctor Parnassus is the 1,000-year-old leader of a traveling theater troupe, and the movie's plot revolves around the latest of his ongoing bets with the devil, as personified by Mr. Nick (Tom Waits). Gilliam uses as his central dramatic device the magical mirror that is the leading attraction of Parnassus's road show: Ledger's Tony character escorts audience members *through* the mirror and into various fantasy worlds of their own devising.

At the time of Heath Ledger's death, Gilliam had already shot all the "real world" scenes in which the actor is featured. The director decided that his movie could be credibly completed were he to use three separate actors to play the Tony character during its three "through the mirror" sequences. The first candidate that came to the director's mind was Johnny Depp, the man who had been booked to play one of the lead roles in Gilliam's ill-fated *Don Quixote* film.

Depp, who had been a friend of Ledger's, had no hesitation in agreeing to join the cast of *Doctor Parnassus*. Gilliam got

Left: The clifftop gallows where Tony meets his end, Parnassus having traded him to the devil in return for the soul of his daughter.

Above: Imaginarium Tony 1 (Depp) escorts a woman (Maggie Steed) wearing Louis Vuitton on a journey into her imagination.

similarly positive responses from Jude Law and Colin Farrell, both of whom could count themselves among the Australian actor's acquaintances. The three substitute actors would respectively be billed as Imaginarium Tonys 1, 2, and 3. Filming was scheduled to resume in Vancouver in late February of 2008, at which point Johnny Depp was near Chicago, making *Public Enemies* with Michael Mann.

Circumstances dictated that Depp could make himself available to Gilliam for no more than 27 hours, so the director knew the actor would have only one take each time the cameras started rolling. It is a testament to Depp's professionalism that this constraint is not apparent during any of his time on screen in the finished movie. After Ledger accompanies a middle-aged woman though Doctor Parnassus's magical mirror, Depp takes over as a white-suited, pony-tailed gigolo type; when "Tony 1" briefly catches his own reflection in an everyday mirror he recoils in disbelief, setting a nicely self-deprecating tone for his supplemental scene.

The traumatic circumstances of the film's creation meant that when it was shown at festivals in late 2009, *The Imaginarium of*

*Doctor Parnassus* received significantly greater media attention than one might normally expect for a movie so quintessentially Gilliam-esque. The film is a psychedelic fever-dream that somehow manages not to lose sight of its emotional core amid the director's riotous feedback-loop of arcane surrealism, although it is clearly not designed to appeal to anyone unfamiliar with Gilliam's previous work. If anything, the death of Heath Ledger seemed to make viewers consciously appraise the movie without sentimentality—nonetheless, the verdict on Terry Gilliam's latest offering was largely favorable. (Given Gilliam's well-established proclivity for the peculiar, few journalists were surprised to hear him say that certain aspects of the 1,000-year-old Parnassus character were autobiographical.)

At the 2010 Oscars, *The Imaginarium of Doctor Parnassus* received two nominations, for Best Art Direction and Best Costume Design, although it did not win in either category. All three of the actors who were called on to depict Ledger's character in the film donated their fees to the actor's infant daughter, who had not been born when his will was drawn up several years earlier.

# Public Enemies

2009

"John Dillinger was that era's rock 'n' roll star. He was a very charismatic man and he lived the way he wanted to and didn't compromise."

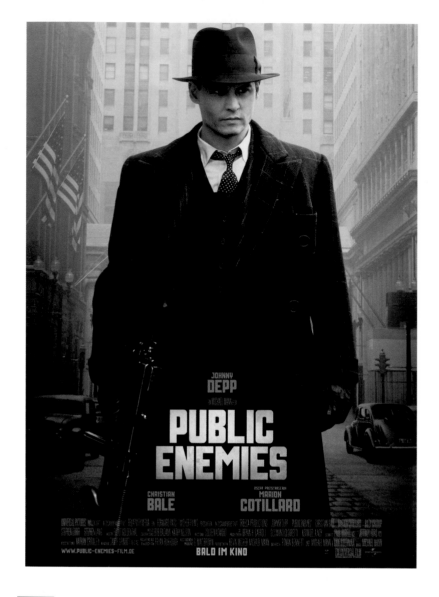

This twenty-first century take on legendary 1930s gangster John Dillinger is directed by Michael Mann, using as his principal source the lavishly praised 2004 work *Public Enemies: America's Greatest Crime Wave and the Birth of the FBI, 1933–34*, written by Bryan Burrough of *Vanity Fair* magazine. The book's subtitle may have been more suggestive of a multi-part PBS/BBC documentary, but the prospect of Mann as director and Johnny Depp as leading man convinced Universal that basing a $100 million movie on it was a reasonable bet.

Johnny Depp plays it ice-cool as Dillinger, as he has done in practically every role that's helped establish him as one of the preeminent actors of his era. Depp's mode comes in sharp contrast to the previous big-screen portrayal of the gangster, John Milius's 1973 film *Dillinger*, in which Warren Oates depicted the title character as a gregarious, wise-cracking charmer with folk-wisdom to burn. While Depp's interpretation of Dillinger carries far more authority than Oates's, and will better withstand the test of time, it doesn't really make for a particularly captivating central character.

Just after the film opened, Depp told London's *Daily Telegraph* that "John Dillinger was that era's rock and roll star. He was a very charismatic man and he lived the way he wanted to and didn't compromise." Although Depp's Dillinger has the odd snappy one-liner, and carries out the occasional act of ruthless bravado, it's hard to discern anything of the rock star about him; in fact one can't help but suspect that the character must be hiding something from us. Yet judging by historical accounts, this is a character who didn't actually have a great deal to conceal; what you saw was what you got. It turns out that Depp may be giving the game away early in the film when he flatly intones, "I'm John Dillinger—I rob banks."

Dillinger was only one of the numerous protagonists in Bryan Burrough's book, which was not built around detailed biographies of individual Depression-era criminals, or theories about what motivated them. Instead Burrough examined the way in which these characters collectively initiated a national crime wave large enough to transform the Federal Bureau of Investigation into the bureaucratic juggernaut that is still with

Business and pleasure:
The notorious bank-robber
John Dillinger pulls off
another heist and waltzes
away with girlfriend Billie
Frechette (Marion Cotillard).

us to this day. Of course, no film director would be forging a compelling movie narrative from such a complex story—least of all Michael Mann.

Depp's chief accomplice in *Public Enemies* is the French actress Marion Cotillard (as Dillinger's girlfriend Billie Frechette), who shares a few genuinely tender scenes with him in between the movie's overblown shoot-outs. The movie is also bolstered by the presence of the underrated Billy Crudup, whose portrayal of the Machiavellian FBI boss J. Edgar Hoover has an archly sardonic undertone. However, in the larger role of Melvin Purvis, the FBI man charged with apprehending Dillinger, Christian Bale is atypically anonymous. Still, at least Purvis manages to have the last word in his frustrating personal battle with Dillinger, because he's part of the law-enforcement team that guns down the storied bank-robber in front of Chicago's Biograph Theater, where Dillinger has been taking in a gangster flick.

Johnny Depp has never looked better than he does in *Public Enemies*—and, paradoxically enough, that is one of the central

problems with Mann's film. Depp may have been born just a few hours' drive from his character's home town of East Chicago, Indiana, but it's hard to think of a 1930s movie star with exotic looks comparable to Depp's. And even in the world of small-time hoods (which is what Dillinger was, despite his outsize reputation), John Dillinger's physical appearance was nothing to write home about. No one would be naïve enough to expect total verisimilitude in a movie biography, but in this case the very presence of Johnny Depp makes it just a little harder to believe that *Public Enemies'* hyperkinetic narrative could be taking place during America's Great Depression.

This temporal dissonance is compounded by Michael Mann's obsession with visual style above all else: The banks that Dillinger robs are infinitely grander than the shabby establishments where he actually plied his felonious trade; not to mention the fact that this is a director who—as many critics noted—seems to have no interest in even hinting at the kind of financial hardship that most Americans were suffering during the Depression. Mann's one nod to the economic

*"I feel he was kind of a Robin Hood because he truly cared about people. He knew time was short and I believe he had found himself and was at peace with the fact that it wasn't going to be a very long ride, but it was going to be a significant ride."*

Opposite: "I'm John Dillinger—I rob banks."

Above: FBI agent Melvin Purvis (Christian Bale) has Dillinger behind bars, but not for long.

conditions prevalent during Dillinger's 14-month crime spree is the observation that the gangster's antics had widespread support among an embattled population that had come to hate its nation's banking system as a whole.

*Public Enemies* is clearly the product of a director concerned with being "visually stylish" above all else, and Michael Mann's name has been synonymous with those two words since he created *Miami Vice*, the smash-hit TV cop show that was launched in 1984 and—over the course of five seasons—became regarded as one of the definitive culture-products of its surface-obsessed decade. Mann's reputation continued to grow apace over subsequent decades, despite the fact that most of his output could be adequately summed up in two, rather more straightforward words: "technically impressive."

Mann's counterintuitive decision to shoot *Public Enemies* digitally, often via handheld HD cameras, gives the film the jolting, low-budget immediacy of a modern-day "reality" television show, or live news coverage of some protracted crime in progress. "I didn't want people to watch it from a distance,"

Mann explained at the time of the film's release. "I wanted them to have an intimate connection to those times and for those times to have an impact on people." Unfortunately, *Public Enemies'* crisp, ultra-bright visual style tends to have an alienating effect on the viewer—which may be among the factors that contributed to the film's lukewarm performance at the box office. Although its reviews were largely respectable, *Public Enemies* brought in a worldwide total of $215 million, which looks like an impressive figure to anyone who does not know the financial expectations that accompany a budget of $100 million.

The relative commercial failure of *Public Enemies* didn't quite make Michael Mann a public enemy in Hollywood, but it only served to exacerbate the serious damage done to his reputation by the abject failure of his bombastic 2006 *Miami Vice* movie—Mann's next job took him back to television, as director of the Showtime series *Luck* (starring Dustin Hoffman). Actors are generally held less immediately accountable for the vagaries of public taste, none less so than Johnny Depp, who once again bounced back in a most unexpected way.

# Alice in Wonderland

2010

..................

"If you're not walking on a tightrope, juggling super-sharp knives, there's really no reason to do it."

The notion of Tim Burton directing a new film adaptation of Lewis Carroll's 1865 children's classic *Alice's Adventures in Wonderland* may have seemed perfectly obvious to anyone familiar with the director's work, but the project did not actually originate with him. *Alice* was actually brought to Burton by screenwriter/novelist Linda Woolverton, who had decided to merge *Alice's Adventures in Wonderland* and the 1871 sequel, *Through the Looking-Glass*, into a single story, and to add some new twists to Lewis Carroll's now-familiar vision. *Alice* saw Burton embracing the twenty-first-century trend of releasing films in 3D, but his decision to film in 2D and add a dimension in post-production angered James "Avatar" Cameron, who accused his directorial colleague of "stunting 3D growth"—whatever that might mean.

In narrative terms, Burton's *Alice* would not be a young girl, but a 19 year old beating a retreat from the pressures of the encroaching adult world; and she would not end up in Wonderland, but in "Underland," a version of Carroll's unsettling fantasy world that is—despite being warped in several new directions—still instantly recognizable. (Toward the end of the film, one of the Underland characters makes a reference to Alice's childhood visit to that surreal domain and her misinterpretation of its name as "Wonderland.")

In putting together *Alice*'s ensemble cast, Burton handed the title role to the little-known Australian actress Mia Wasikowska, who was 18 when she got the role; the director gave key supporting parts to two extremely familiar faces. Helena Bonham Carter—with whom the director now had two children—would play the tyrannical Red Queen; while the ever-reliable Johnny Depp—the godfather to both of Burton and Bonham Carter's children—would feature as Alice's frenetic tour guide the Mad Hatter.

Unlike so many of Depp's characters in previous movies, his new version of the Mad Hatter was not primarily inspired

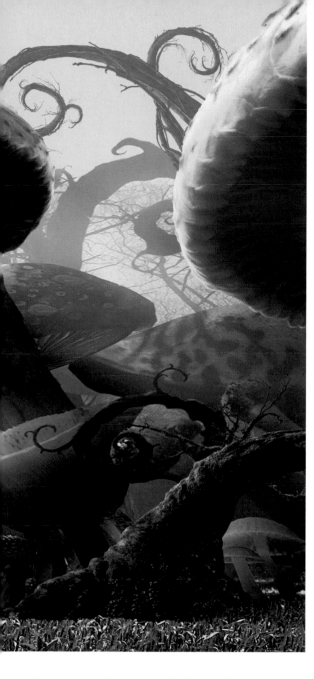

Left: Depp's Mad Hatter owes his insanity to mercury poisoning rather than magic mushrooms.

Below: Johnny Depp and Tim Burton are once again on the same page.

*"One time, Tim and I were talking before we were getting ready to shoot. Afterwards, one of the grips comes over to me with this really perplexed look on his face. He says, 'I was just watching you and Tim talk about the scene for the last 15 minutes.' 'Yeah?' And he says, 'I didn't understand a fucking word either one of you said.'"*

by any combination of other individuals (either fictional or real) but by a lesser-known component of English life in the mid-nineteenth century. The felt with which milliners of the period lined their hats was manufactured using a process that involved mercury; and when the substance leeched through the skin of these hat-makers it often caused mental problems.

When Johnny Depp discovered this nugget of information he decided to extrapolate upon it, and create a Mad Hatter truly worthy of the name. "I think [he] was poisoned—very, very poisoned," said Depp. "And I think it just took effect in all his nerves."

Since the behavior of Carroll's outlandish character may well have been caused by exposure to mercury, Depp opted simply to exaggerate the symptoms of one of the resulting conditions and let his mentally disturbed character jump erratically between multiple personalities, one of which had a distinct Glasgow accent. (And of a most unexpected provenance: Depp used the

popular Scottish comedy character Rab C. Nesbitt as the basis.) In a bit of business that would almost certainly be overlooked by anyone lacking a degree in Lewis Carroll Studies, Depp made sure that his gap-toothed Mad Hatter also displayed external symptoms of mercury poisoning: which is why his skin has an orange glow, and why an orange substance appears to be oozing from his cuticles and his skin.

Johnny Depp's Mad Hatter even has orange, curly hair extruding from beneath his signature top hat—the actor gives an insanely mannered performance that perfectly suits the antic nature of Tim Burton's reinterpretation of the *Alice* mythos. Burton's work often has its roots in the sketches he makes to develop his cinematic visions; it is then channeled through the sensibility of his inner set designer, a process that wins him many fans while providing fodder for critics. With *Alice in Wonderland* the inner set designer is running the show: There's an appropriately nauseating giddiness to the

movie, produced by the way Burton manages to bombard his audience with perverse visual treats. The most memorable of these, of course, is the computer-generated effect that gives Helena Bonham Carter's bratty Red Queen a bulbous, oversized head atop a grotesquely petite frame.

One defining characteristic of Lewis Carroll's *Alice* books is the teeming cast of characters that passes through them, so by opting to play the Mad Hatter, Johnny Depp was knowingly subsuming his *Pirates of the Caribbean* star power for the greater good. Depp was only one of three actors featured on posters for *Alice in Wonderland* (Bonham Carter and Wasikowska were the other two), but the film's financial performance would offer at least some indication as to the ongoing viability of the creative alliance Burton and Depp first forged 20 years earlier. Once again there were mixed reviews—and once again a Burton/Depp project did terrific business, this time joining the second *Pirates* movie in the $1 billion-plus category.

Above left: "What a regrettably large head you have." Thanks to CGI manipulation Helena Bonham Carter is barely recognizable as the Red Queen.

Above: A diminished Alice (Mia Wasikowska) joins the Mad Hatter's frabjous tea party.

"To choose to grab Alice in Wonderland, *that in itself is one thing,* and then to do it to the Tim Burton level is madness. It's so huge because, whether it's the CGI or the green screen or the 3D or the live action, he's done it all here. It's the greatest undertaking I've heard of."

# The Tourist

2010

.................

"It's tougher to play someone like my character in *The Tourist*. I have the most fun when I can hide behind wigs or hats or makeup."

The "Tourist" Frank Tupelo (Johnny Depp) takes in the sights of Venice and makes a getaway with British agent Elise Clifton-Ward (Angelina Jolie).

This re-make of the 2005 French thriller *Anthony Zimmer* did not get off to the most auspicious of starts, with a series of abrupt personnel changes afflicting the project before production commenced in February 2010. By that point director Florian Henckel von Donnersmarck had quit the project over "creative differences," then returned to rewrite the final version of the script in two weeks. Henckel von Donnersmarck made his name as the director of the peerless 2006 cold-war thriller *The Lives of Others* (which won the Oscar for Best Foreign Language Film in 2007), and it would be hard to imagine a less appropriate follow-up for him than *The Tourist*.

The last-minute rewriting of *The Tourist*'s script can only have exacerbated the short deadline imposed on the film by Johnny Depp's pre-existing commitments to the *Pirates of the Caribbean* franchise. *The Tourist* was shot in just under two months, an astoundingly brief period for a film with a budget of $100 million. Unfortunately, the circumstances of its creation were only too evident in the final product.

Depp's physical appearance in *The Tourist* recalls the near-forgotten 1995 thriller *Nick of Time*, in which he took the

opportunity to add a rare "normal guy" to his growing collection of freaks and geeks. This time Depp plays a character named Frank Tupelo, whom we first see on a Paris-to-Venice train, looking dowdier, far less hip, and rather more jowly than the Johnny Depp we'd become accustomed to over the years. Tupelo is quickly joined by a glamorous stranger named Elise Clifton-Ward (Angelina Jolie), whom we already know to be a British law-enforcement official involved in a high-tech mission to apprehend a villainous ex-boyfriend. Jolie dusts off the posh English accent she used in the title role of the lukewarm 2001 video-game adaptation *Lara Croft: Tomb Raider*, and aggressively sets about casting a spell over her slow-witted American companion.

Director Florian Henckel von Donnersmarck reassures the audience that it is watching a big-league movie by revealing that Elise Clifton-Ward's former beau, Alexander Pearce, is wanted by Scotland Yard over the matter of £744 million in unpaid taxes. And to confirm that this will be a complex and intriguing thriller, we hear that Pearce has spent $20 million on making himself unrecognizable via plastic surgery. And as though that

weren't enough, it transpires that Pearce has purloined some £2 billion from the English crime lord Reginald Shaw (Steven Berkoff)—Shaw has been informed of Jolie's trip to Venice, and plans to intercept her there in an effort to find Alexander Pearce.

While a film like *The Tourist* is not expected to be overly concerned with realism or earth-bound logic, in order to achieve its dramatic aims it must retain at least some level of plausibility. This is something that Henckel von Donnersmarck does not seem to acknowledge, so the cracks are already beginning to show when Clifton-Ward invites Frank Tupelo to share her accommodations. Alarm bells start ringing when, for the second time in the film, this exotic (and quite possibly dangerous) lady receives an anonymous note dictating her next move, and obeys it.

What follows is an undifferentiated mélange of abductions, arrests, boat chases, sniper fire, and double- (possibly triple-) crossing which somehow combines to precious little effect, even when you factor in the Major Twist that comes at the very end of the film. The only real intrigue created by *The Tourist* is, how did Johnny Depp end up appearing in it? (At that stage

in his career, it's doubtful that a fee of $20 million alone would have been enough to secure Depp's signature.) One might also have asked how any film could be so utterly wrong-headed, given the involvement of such high-ranking co-writers as Julian Fellowes (*Gosford Park*) and Christopher McQuarrie (*The Usual Suspects*)—however, Fellowes revealed that the final movie contained very little of his input.

As one would imagine, when *The Tourist* was released in December 2010 it did not go down well with critics—to say the least. The general consensus on this would-be blockbuster was neatly summed up by Peter Travers of *Rolling Stone*; Travers is known as one of the more charitable major movie reviewers in the US, but on this occasion he snarled, "*The Tourist* reaches its own kind of perfection—it fails on every conceivable level." American cinema-goers stayed away in their droves, and the film earned a disappointing $67 million domestically; however, with overseas revenue of $210 million, this artistic aberration did not have to bear the additional stigma of being a commercial disaster.

The whole debacle would probably have blown over by early 2011 had the Hollywood Foreign Press Association

"Angelina is kind of a walking poem— the perfect beauty who at the same time is very deep and very smart."

Left: Depp and Jolie dance the tango, but their footwork was not quick enough to avoid a drubbing by the critics and a ribbing by Golden Globes host Ricky Gervais.

Opposite: Attending the German premiere of *The Tourist*, Berlin, December 2010.

(HFPA) not decided to include *The Tourist* in its Golden Globe nominations—in the "Best Motion Picture: Musical or Comedy" category. When the nominees were announced, the *Hollywood Reporter* aired one popular theory about *The Tourist*'s bizarre re-classification: "Think of this as a particularly elaborate engraved invitation" [for Depp and Jolie to attend the awards ceremony]. The HFPA hastily pointed out that the whole thing had been the idea of *The Tourist*'s producers and its director.

While *The Tourist* was not without its moments of intentional drollery, the HFPA had effectively transformed the film itself into a cultural punch line. To make matters worse, the 2011 Golden Globe awards were presented by English comedian Ricky Gervais, who had run roughshod over Tinseltown decorum during the previous year's ceremony by dishing out insults to several rich and powerful attendees, including Mel Gibson. This year Johnny Depp and Angelina Jolie (both nominated in the same ill-fitting category as *The Tourist* itself) would be among those on the receiving end.

Within two minutes of opening up the Golden Globes ceremony, Gervais remarked on the number of successful 3D movies that had appeared in 2010. "It seems like everything this year was three-dimensional," he added, "except the characters in

*The Tourist*... I'm jumping on the bandwagon, because I haven't even seen *The Tourist*. Who has?"

Gervais carried on swinging: "I'd like to quash the rumors that the only reason *The Tourist* was nominated was so that the Hollywood Foreign Press can hang out with Johnny Depp and Angelina Jolie. That is rubbish, that is not the only reason— they also accepted bribes." Cut to Johnny Depp, sitting in the audience, chewing gum, and grinning gamely.

No one in Hollywood could have been more immune to Ricky Gervais' barbs than Depp, whose hot streak resumed just a few months after the Golden Globes with the acclaimed animated feature *Rango* and the barnstorming fourth installment of the *Pirates of the Caribbean* saga. But toward the end of the year, Depp reignited the painful saga of *The Tourist* with a gesture that few A-list actors would even consider: He appeared as himself in an episode of Gervais' HBO discomfort-comedy series *Life's Too Short*. After striding into Gervais' office, Depp drops a lit cigarette into the comedian's water glass before unleashing, in an apparent state of agitation, a flurry of Ricky Gervais gags. Opinion was divided on whether the scene, from Depp's point of view, represented a triumph or a further humiliation—which may well have been exactly the kind of reaction he'd been hoping for.

# Pirates of the Caribbean
## On Stranger Tides

2011

"It's been a gas, it's been a gas, and the whole experience has been… I mean there's not a bad thing you can say about it."

> "*This one is a little closer in tone to the first, more character driven… more subject driven. It has a freshness and less mathematics.*"

In May 2011, just prior to the release of the fourth film in the rampaging *Pirates of the Caribbean* series, Johnny Depp made the following confession in the pages of *Entertainment Weekly*: "I remember talking to [director Gore Verbinski] at certain points during production of [*Pirates*] 2 or 3 and saying, 'I don't really know what this means.' He said, 'Neither do I, but let's just shoot it.'" What is even more jaw-dropping than Depp's statement about his money-spinning maritime franchise is that, despite the leading man admitting that even he couldn't unravel its plotlines, the most impenetrable of the three films— *At World's End*, the third in the series—still earned almost a billion dollars in worldwide box-office revenue, as well as the untold millions generated by its countless marketing angles. The intriguing question was, after being baffled by the loopy logic of the third *Pirates* film, would the public come back for a fourth serving? As much as anything, the answer would reveal a lot about the current wattage of Johnny Depp's star power.

The money men behind the *Pirates* series appeared to be hedging their bets on the fourth film's commercial prospects, given their openness about the decision to make the new picture on a budget somewhat smaller than the amount that had been spent on *At World's End*. Fiscal prudence meant that cheaper locations were chosen for *On Stranger Tides*, and that there were shorter schedules for production and (more drastically) for post-production. Due to the latter time-compression, special effects duties were farmed out to no fewer than 10 different companies.

There were just two items on the budget for *On Stranger Tides* on which no expense was spared. With *Chicago* director Rob Marshall replacing Gore Verbinski at the helm, the new film was shot in 3D, with upgraded versions of the cameras that James Cameron used on his groundbreaking 2009 smash *Avatar*. And while Disney balked at Johnny Depp's request to be given a percentage of box-office revenue for his fourth portrayal of Captain Jack Sparrow, the company reportedly agreed to pay him a record-breaking $55 million for his labors.

Financial concerns aside, it was decreed that the fourth *Pirates* film had to be reined in creatively, since *At World's End* had taken almost three hours to tell its unfathomable tale.

This meant that Captain Jack's latest adventure would be a stand-alone story that precluded the kind of scattershot thinking that left behind so much confusion and so many loose ends when the initial trilogy had run its course. In further acknowledgment that Johnny Depp's presence was the one irreplaceable component of this new, multi-billion dollar subset of the movie industry, the producers of *On Stranger Tides* granted him a significant degree of input into the film's script.

Since the third *Pirates* installment ended with a definite conclusion to the stories of Elizabeth Swann (Keira Knightley) and Will Turner (Orlando Bloom), both of those primary characters could clearly be dispensed with. As far back as 2007, the series' principal writers Terry Rossio and Ted Elliott had come across Tim Powers' 1987 pirate novel *On Stranger Tides*, which Disney quietly optioned. By turning to the book as a source for the fourth *Pirates* outing, the movie's creators found the basis for two new characters to place alongside Jack Sparrow. The first of these was the legendary villain Blackbeard, who is portrayed in the movie by the grizzled

English actor Ian McShane (best known to US audiences as Al Swearengen, the central character in HBO's acclaimed three-season drama *Deadwood*).

*On Stranger Tides*' other new character is Blackbeard's daughter Angelica, an ex-lover of Captain Jack's who is limned by Johnny Depp's *Blow* co-star Penélope Cruz. The star-crossed pair meet in the most preposterous circumstance: a sword-fight instigated by Sparrow when he sees someone trying to pass themselves off as him in a dockside tavern. After a few minutes of clashing steel, Captain Jack pulls off the stranger's false moustache to reveal... Angelica, whom he cruelly deserted some years before.

The pugnacious wench exacts a measure of revenge for Jack's betrayal by tricking him into joining her father's quest for the mythical Fountain of Youth, where they must enact a complex, chalice-related ritual for reasons that are not entirely clear. Jack's plight is particularly unfortunate since he has just expended a great deal of energy escaping from his old rival Barbossa, who is now in the employ of King George II (played

"*I think, for me, because I love the character so much, and I enjoy playing the character so much and people seem to like it, if there's an opportunity to try again, you know, it's like going up to bat. You want to get back out there and try and try and try and see what you can do. I enjoy playing Captain Jack very much.*"

Above: The moment when Jack comes face to face with his imposter.

Opposite: King George II attempts to enlist Captain Jack to find the Fountain of Youth on his behalf.

Overleaf: Rowing away from Angelica but not from the franchise—Depp has signed up for a fifth *Pirates* installment.

by Richard Griffiths at his foppish best) and—thanks to the ever-glowering Blackbeard—sporting a wooden leg. Barbossa is also intent on reaching the Fountain of Youth, and wants Jack to help him get there ahead of the Spanish fleet.

As played by Geoffrey Rush, Barbossa is given more prominence in *On Stranger Tides* than he had in previous episodes, and he is allowed to deliver a fair number of the regular one-line zingers that had hitherto been the sole property of Depp's character. This shift in personal dynamics gives the film a lift, as does the highly charged relationship between Angelica and Jack Sparrow; the value of these two new factors increases as the film's screenwriters start weaving a tapestry of barely plausible plotlines, and laboriously inserting outlandish new elements, chief among them being a gang of homicidal mermaids, most of whom wouldn't look out of place in an eighteenth-century, aquatic version of the Victoria's Secret catalogue.

The film's climax occurs with a showdown at the Fountain of Youth, which results in a bloody and supernatural demise for

one of its protagonists. In the wake of that dizzying interlude, the movie ends on a quiet note, with Jack and Angelica alone on a small desert island. She declares her eternal love for him; he responds by hastily rowing away and leaving her stranded—with only a Jack Sparrow voodoo doll for company...

Despite its failure to deliver on its creators' promises of narrative coherence, *On Stranger Tides* is certainly more concise and less convoluted than its immediate predecessor. The critical response to the movie, however, was less than favorable, with many reviewers complaining of Sparrow-fatigue and accusing the *Pirates* series of outliving its welcome. Yet, as so often happens, the public did not concur, and the fourth installment of *Pirates of the Caribbean* went on to earn more than $1 billion worldwide, becoming the ninth highest-grossing film of all time. Johnny Depp's box-office mojo was still apparently working; although it was slightly unsettling to note that the ascendancy of his appeal in overseas markets was threatening to turn him into that most derided subspecies of actor, the "international superstar."

"*If they want to keep me in the part and roll me out in years to come as Jack in a wheelchair, I'll be up for it.*"

# The Rum Diary

2011
....................

"I believe that
this film will have
a shelf life. I think
it will stick around
and people will watch
it and enjoy it."

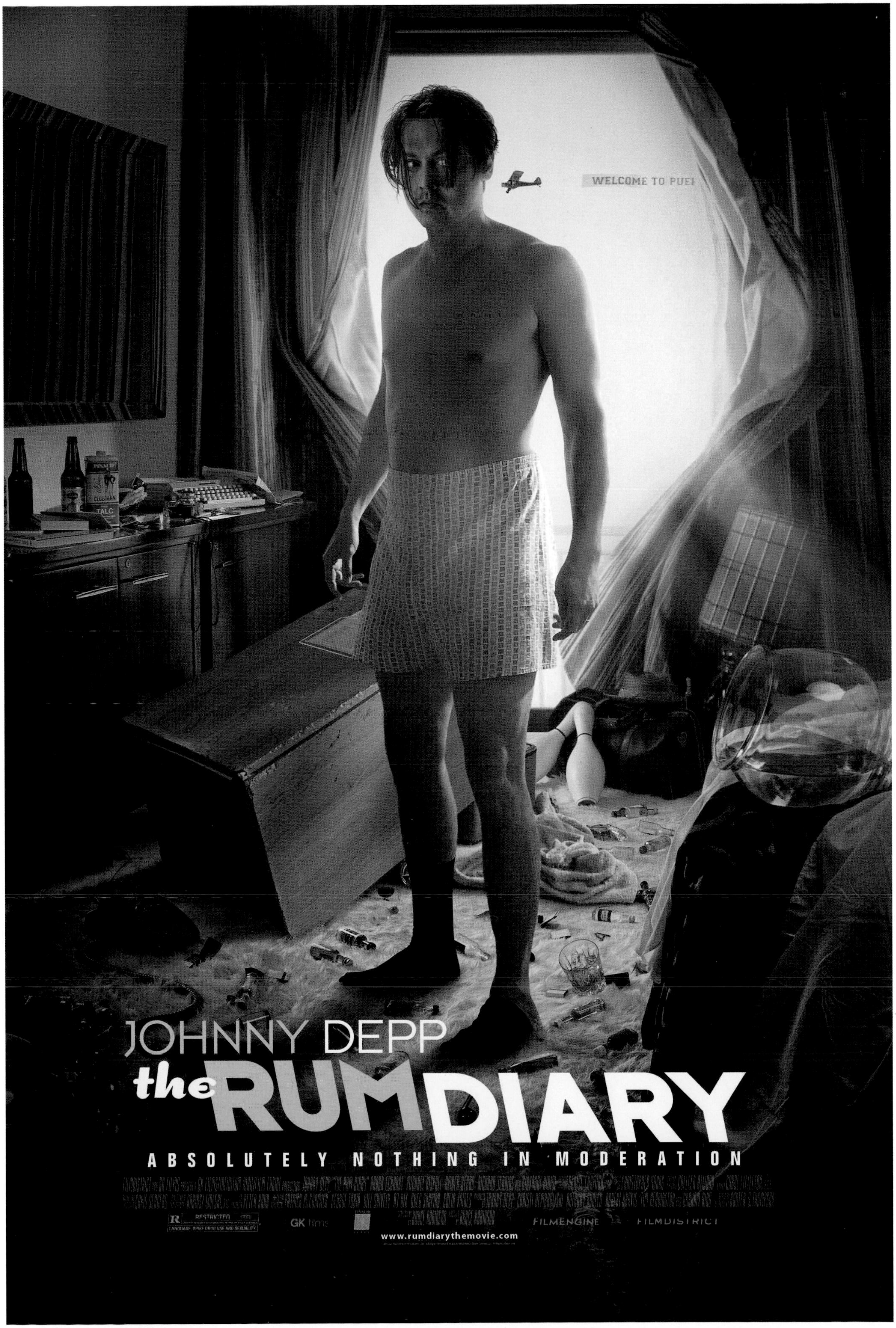

WELCOME TO PUE
CLUBMAN
TALC
JOHNNY DEPP
the RUM DIARY
ABSOLUTELY NOTHING IN MODERATION
R RESTRICTED
GK films
FILMENGINE
FILMDISTRICT
www.rumdiarythemovie.com

"*When we were filming* The Rum Diary, *Hunter was a presence, you know. We had a chair on the set with his name on it. We had a bottle of Chivas Regal, a highball glass filled with ice, his Dunhills and cigarette holder.*"

Left: Thirteen years after *Fear and Loathing in Las Vegas*, Depp plays Paul Kemp, another version of Hunter S. Thompson.

Opposite top: An on-set discussion with director Bruce Robinson.

Opposite bottom: The hard-living Kemp has a candlelit drinking session with fellow journalists Sala (Michael Rispoli) and Moberg (Giovanni Ribisi).

Six years after the death of his good friend and comrade Hunter S. Thompson, Johnny Depp made good on their plans to realize a movie version of Thompson's semi-autobiographical novel *The Rum Diary*, written in the early sixties and finally published in 1998. As one might expect, Depp took on the role of Paul Kemp, a thinly veiled version of the young Thompson, who ventures from New York to Puerto Rico to bluff his way onto the island's main English-language newspaper, the *San Juan Star*.

The process began with Depp setting himself a not-inconsiderable challenge: He decided that the only writer-director suited to this project was Bruce Robinson, the sardonic and reclusive Englishman who'd entered a state of semi-retirement nearly two decades earlier, aged 46. Robinson is best known as the creator of *Withnail and I* (1987), which belongs to the small and exalted group of films (see also *The Big Lebowski*) whose cult following seems only to expand from year to year, and whose True Believers impute the work with an almost religious significance. It's hard to imagine a single living actor who could have persuaded Bruce Robinson to leave his remote farmhouse to direct his first film in 19 years, so it speaks volumes for Depp's sincere charm that he somehow managed to achieve that very goal.

Drawn from Thompson's personal experience of a brief 1960 work sojourn to Puerto Rico, *The Rum Diary* begins with Depp's Paul Kemp character getting hired at the *San Juan Star* after its editor ridicules his résumé as a work of blatant fiction. This apparent act of kindness is explained when Kemp finds out that he was the sole applicant for the job. Much to his consternation and bemusement, he realizes that he has just

Sharing a moment with Chenault (Amber Heard), the trophy wife-to-be of ruthless realtor Sanderson (above); and taking in one of Puerto Rico's deserted beaches (left).

Johnny Depp and Amber Heard at a *Rum Diary* photocall, Paris, November 2011.

joined a ramshackle operation staffed by indolent misfits, plus the handful of veteran pressmen who actually do all the work involved in putting out a daily newspaper.

Thanks to Bruce Robinson's astute editing of the young Thompson's scrappy novel, the prevailing mood of *The Rum Diary* is redolent of the Graham Greene stories that effortlessly juxtapose colonial dissipation and misrule with simmering resentment among the native populace. As a newcomer to Puerto Rico, Paul Kemp is particularly sensitive to the sociopolitical climate he finds there, but a hefty drinking habit keeps him well insulated from such unpalatable realities. *The Rum Diary*—$45 million budget notwithstanding—is a movie that seems to be consciously limited in its scope, although Johnny Depp's performance would grace any of Hollywood's smartest nine-figure political thrillers. Having played the older, more cynical, and drug-damaged version of Thompson in *Fear and Loathing in Las Vegas* in 1998, Depp manages to reverse-engineer that self-destructive character into a younger man who evinces subtle yet unmistakable traces of what he'll become within little more than a decade.

A Gatsby-esque real-estate macher named Sanderson (played by Aaron Eckhart) recruits Kemp into a circle of venal associates who expect him to trade his journalistic integrity—such as it is—for hard cash, and concoct stories that will benefit their schemes to transform the region into their own lucrative fiefdom. Kemp hazily comprehends that this represents a critical juncture in his life; however, the ethical hand-wringing is put on hold as he copes with the problems created by the insidiously flirtatious attentions of Sanderson's alluring and alarmingly young fiancée, Chenault, played by the twentysomething Texan actress Amber Heard.

Despite the evident modesty of its ambitions, *The Rum Diary* received particularly unkind treatment from film critics. Then again, the fact that Depp had enjoyed commercial success with badly reviewed films in the past suggests that the abject failure of this project may have been caused by Hollywood's most virulent disease: bad word of mouth. So Bruce Robinson's comeback was quickly forgotten—although this would not be the last time that Johnny Depp's name appeared in print next to that of his youthful co-star Amber Heard.

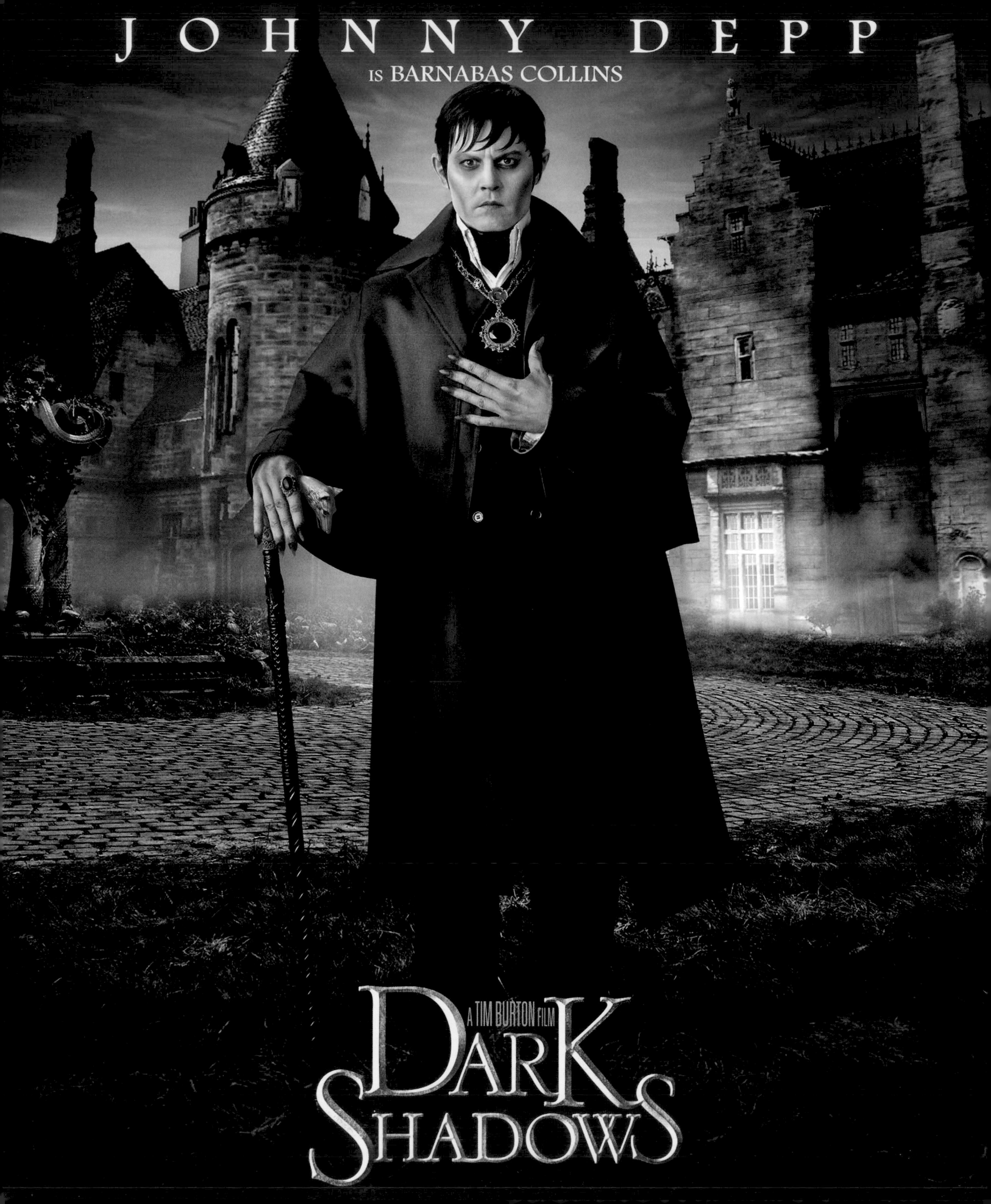
JOHNNY DEPP
IS BARNABAS COLLINS
A TIM BURTON FILM
DARK
SHADOWS

# Dark Shadows

2012

.....................

"It was an opportunity... to sort of go into what really doesn't exist so much anymore, which is classic monster makeup and a classic monster character."

The year 2012 found Tim Burton bellying up once more to the re-make buffet—only this time he was addressing a project of an entirely different stripe from his reinterpretations of *Planet of the Apes* and *Charlie and the Chocolate Factory*. Wiser heads within the film business tend to believe that there are two valid reasons for re-making a movie: either the original film represented the flawed execution of a strong idea; or it was not— for one reason or another—fully appreciated in its own time. (The question of creating English-language versions of foreign films seems to occupy a gray area somewhere between this category and the updating of hit movies from the past.)

The original *Dark Shadows* was a true cultural mutation that didn't quite fit into any existing paradigm: This was a Gothic-tinged, 30-minute afternoon drama that hit its stride only when, after an unsuccessful launch, it turned in desperation to supernatural storylines. Despite being denounced as "Satan's favorite TV show" by at least one religious group, this second incarnation of *Dark Shadows* thrived, ultimately racking up 1,225 episodes between 1966 and 1971.

While this profoundly odd series has faded from the mass memory, it still has its devotees, including both Tim Burton and Johnny Depp, the latter of whom—despite being only just old enough to have remembered the show during its original run— initially had the idea of doing a film adaptation. After Depp managed to persuade his old friend to collaborate with him on a *Dark Shadows* movie, Burton's own enthusiasm for the series took over, and he brought TV writer Seth Grahame-Smith on board to flesh out his vision for the project.

*Dark Shadows*, like its television precursor, revolves around a dandy-ish vampire named Barnabas Collins—only the movie version, which is set in 1972, features a 200-year-old version of the character, who is accidentally disinterred by an unfortunate construction crew. Barnabas's haughty reaction to unfamiliar modernity suggests an exaggerated version of Austin Powers; or perhaps an extension of the central conceit behind *Adam Adamant Lives!*, the 1960s British TV series in which an Edwardian gent is thawed out in Swinging London after spending 64 years encased in a block of ice.

"*There's an elegance to this guy that's kind of fun;
Barnabas is a good one. And just look around—
there's nothing like working with Tim.*"

Barnabas returns to the Collins family mansion in the Maine town of Collinsport and, in the stilted manner of William Shatner doing Shakespeare, acquaints himself with his dysfunctional descendants. Only family matriarch Elizabeth Collins Stoddard (played by a sublimely frosty Michelle Pfeiffer) is privy to Barnabas's 200-year-old secret; to the rest of the family, and all other modern-day persons, he passes himself off as a distant relative who has come from England to revive the family's ailing fishing business.

The Collins' enterprise has been all but eclipsed by a rival operation belonging to Angelique Bouchard (Eva Green), who turns out to be the ageless witch who was responsible for Barnabas becoming a vampire, not to mention his premature burial. Bouchard was motivated by her unreciprocated love for Depp's character, and she gamely makes another attempt to win his affection, this time with a gravity-defying sex scene that is one of several set-piece highlights in *Dark Shadows*.

Eva Green is among several members of Burton's ensemble cast who attain individual excellence in the movie. Aside from Depp and Pfeiffer there is latter-day Burton muse Helena Bonham Carter, who revels in the role of Dr. Julia Hoffman, the blousy in-house shrink who drinks and smokes her way through family dinners. When Hoffman puts Barnabas under hypnosis, she discovers his true identity, which sets in motion a tumultuous chain of soap-operatic events that culminate in arson, an angry mob, and all manner of supernatural mayhem.

Although Tim Burton succeeds in getting sterling performances from his main players, *Dark Shadows*' plot notably fails to gather the kind of momentum one expects from a $150 million movie. Like so many films made by well-established directors in Burton's tax bracket, *Dark Shadows* comes across as the creation of someone who has barely seen a movie, TV show, or magazine in the previous 10 years.

Burton is unable to resist any opportunity to bring the movie's early 1970s backdrop into the foreground, and is unbecomingly excited about having access to all the kitschy delights and trappings of that contentious period, from glitter-balls to glam rock to flammable fabrics. All of which might have been considered hilariously nostalgic had they not been satirized to death over the last two decades. When the third Austin Powers film, *Goldmember*, limped into the 1970s in 2002 it was already many years behind the times—so what chance did *Dark Shadows* have of mining new thrills from that same old decade in May 2012?

Warner Bros. Pictures, which financed *Dark Shadows*, acquired the project in the hope that it would become the kind of franchise film it needed to replace the recently concluded *Harry Potter* series, as well as *Lord of the Rings* and *Batman*, two other major Warner brands that are approaching the end of their lifespans. Burton's film was therefore supported by a big-league promotional effort, accompanied by a media blitz that even managed to place Johnny Depp in the unlikely environs of the daytime talk show *Ellen*.

Sadly for Warner Bros. *Dark Shadows* failed to thrive even in what appeared to be the most vampire-friendly cultural climate in living memory. The film earned a relatively modest $80 million in the US, plus $156 million in foreign markets, which—while not representing a catastrophe, by any means— is not the kind of performance on which franchises are built.

Some pointed to the box-office dominance of the Marvel Comics adaptation *The Avengers* as the undoing of Burton and Depp's latest effort, but a surprisingly solid critical consensus said otherwise. It was generally agreed that *Dark Shadows* lacked focus, and that it was only the gravitas of the ever-dependable Depp that kept the whole thing from fragmenting altogether.

Tim Burton films are always lauded for their visual élan, and this one is no exception; however, at this point such praise was beginning to ring a little hollow. "Storytelling has never been Mr. Burton's specialty," said the *New York Times*' Manohla Dargis in one of the few enthusiastic reviews *Dark Shadows* got in the mainstream media. Some apostates even questioned the ongoing viability of the Depp/Burton alliance, but it remains to be seen whether that particular story has another chapter to it.

**ANIMATED FILMS**

# Corpse Bride

2005
·················

# Rango

2011
·················

On *Rango*:

**"I think it just gives a bunch of grown-ups an opportunity to be silly… It's certainly like nothing I've ever done before, or any of us have ever done before."**

Given that Johnny Depp periodically draws favorable comparison with the silent movie stars of yore, it is mildly ironic that two of his best movies bear no trace of his corporeal presence. The first of Depp's successful forays into the world of feature-length animation was *Corpse Bride*, which Tim Burton worked on during the filming of *Charlie and the Chocolate Factory*. When Depp committed himself to providing a voice for a leading character in *Corpse Bride*, he assumed that he'd begin work on the project after wrapping *Charlie and the Chocolate Factory*. The actor was surprised to discover that his initial recording sessions for the second movie would be taking place in London after long days on the set of Tim Burton's opulent, $150 million extravaganza.

Depp plays *Corpse Bride*'s leading man Victor Van Dort, a pale and hapless fellow whose impoverished "old money" parents have set him up for an arranged marriage to Victoria Everglot (Emily Watson), the offspring of a prominent nouveau-riche couple. During the wedding rehearsal, Victor so badly fluffs his lines that he flees into a nearby forest, where he idly slips the wedding ring onto the root of an old tree. The tree morphs into a voluptuous, blue-tinted creature known only as the Corpse Bride (Helena Bonham Carter), who drags Victor down to the netherworld she now calls home; although its citizens are in various states of physical decay, they are a hedonistic lot, and their subterranean domain provides the location for most of *Corpse Bride*'s musical numbers (written and performed by Tim Burton's long-time musical collaborator Danny Elfman).

The basic narrative of *Corpse Bride*—which Burton co-directed with Mike Johnson—is derived from a nineteenth-century Eastern European folktale that was brought to Tim Burton's attention by his old friend Joe Ranft, a fellow graduate of CalArts. (Ranft was a leading light within the animation studio Pixar at the time of his death in 2005 in a car accident.) Burton decided to set *Corpse Bride* in a non-specific time and place, although he still gave his film an air of distinctly Victorian

*"He didn't feel all that dissimilar to other characters that I've played for Tim. It was just the base emotional feeling. Along the lines of* Scissorhands *is what I felt… He's a bumbling, deeply insecure, nervous character. A lot like me in life."*

repressiveness. The preponderance of British actors in the cast (notably Joanna Lumley, Albert Finney, and Richard E. Grant) probably explains the Anglo-inflected accent Johnny Depp gave to his Victor Van Dort character.

Since Depp didn't have a great deal of time to prepare for his *Corpse Bride* role, he tapped into several characters from his past work, chief among them being Edward Scissorhands. Victor Van Dort may have been only an animated character, but he fitted comfortably into Depp's ever-expanding inventory of "outsider" types. As far back as 1995, Depp described to a *Guardian* interviewer the common thread that runs through so many of the roles he chooses to play, and how he personally connects with that thread. "What interests me is that so-called 'normal' society considers them outcasts, or on the fringe, or oddballs," said Depp. "With any part you play, there's a certain amount of yourself in it. There has to be, otherwise it's not just acting, it's lying. That's not to say I feel different from others. Maybe they have a more difficult time saying: 'I don't feel accepted' or 'I feel

insecure.' These characters are passive: I see them as receivers. I've identified with them since I was very young."

Victor Van Dort's passivity sees him dragged hither and yon by the Corpse Bride until his new underworld acquaintances finally confront their living counterparts in the film's anarchic, but ultimately happy climax. *Corpse Bride* also provided a relatively happy ending for its creators, garnering an Oscar nomination for Best Animated Feature.

The other notable animated film on Johnny Depp's résumé, *Rango*, was made on a far grander scale than the retro-looking *Corpse Bride*. *Rango*'s director, Gore Verbinski, was seeking a change of pace after helming the first three *Pirates* blockbusters, and he initially envisioned the project as a modest, low-budget piece. However, such are the expectations placed upon modern computer-animated movies (particularly those that are crafted by northern California's venerated Industrial Light & Magic) that *Rango* ended up with an immodest budget of $140 million.

Left: In *Rango* Depp provides the voice for the chameleon title character. The movie gave him the chance to work again with Gore Verbinski, director of the first three *Pirates of the Caribbean* episodes.

Opposite: Showing his face at the *Rango* premiere, Los Angeles, February 2011.

Fortunately for Verbinski, his *Pirates* leading man Johnny Depp would also be on board for this new enterprise.

*Rango* opens with a scene that showcases Depp *in excelsis*: The film's titular character—a lonely chameleon with bulging, asymmetrical eyes—puts himself through the vocal warm-up routine of a self-important Shakespearean ac-*tor*, then berates an inanimate troupe of strolling players about their various deficiencies before entering a downward spiral of self-doubt. This action is taking place in the back of an open-topped car, from which Rango and his cohorts are unceremoniously pitched; when they land on a remote desert road, a fleeting visual reference to *Fear and Loathing in Las Vegas* sets the tone for the rest of Verbinski's film.

Like Victor Van Dort before him, Rango amply fulfills the criteria by which Depp judges potential movie roles. The film follows its passive reptilian protagonist on a picaresque adventure through an arid "Old West" that overflows with references to numerous Hollywood classics from the twentieth century. Rango wanders into the benighted, bone-dry burg of Dirt, which is inhabited by an impressive assortment of strange-looking animal species (who are in turn played by an impressive assortment of character actors). A nervous bout of braggadocio gets Rango appointed town sheriff, putting him on a collision course with Dirt's insalubrious Tortoise John (Ned Beatty), whose corrupt scheme to divert the town's water supply sees *Rango* replaying the central theme of Roman Polanski's *Chinatown* on a panoramic scale.

*Rango* won broad acclaim from reviewers, and amassed almost a quarter of a billion dollars in worldwide box-office revenue. Johnny Depp once more found one of his projects entered in the race for Best Animated Feature Oscar, and for once the Academy voted him into the winner's circle.

FROM THE PRODUCER OF **"PIRATES OF THE CARIBBEAN"**

Disney

# THE LONE RANGER

JULY 2013

# Fast Forward

*"I'd actually seen a painting by an artist named Kirby Sattler, and looked at the face of this warrior and thought: That's it. The stripes down the face and across the eyes... it seemed to me like you could almost see the separate sections of the individual, if you know what I mean..."*

By the time director Rob Marshall steered the *Pirates of the Caribbean* series onto the rocks with his blithe and bloated fourth installment, *On Stranger Tides*, much of the franchise's enviable reserve of goodwill had already been tossed overboard like so much ballast. Since the bewitching presence of Johnny Depp was primarily responsible for sustaining 599 minutes of this increasingly random seafaring tetralogy, Depp must surely have harbored some serious concerns about taking on such a burden once again. This may, in turn, explain Disney's willingness to pay its mission-critical star the eye-watering sum of $116 million (plus significant profit participation) to apply the eyeliner for a fifth time.

Well before *Pirates 5* lurches over the horizon, Depp will star in another big-budget feature of intriguing provenance. *The Lone Ranger* is deeply embedded in America's cultural fabric, having started out as a radio series in the 1930s before reemerging in 1949 as a long-running TV show; sadly, the big screen has proved to be an unhappy hunting ground for the wholesome equestrian crime-fighter over the course of many decades. The 2013 *Lone Ranger* reunites Depp with original *Pirates* director, Gore Verbinski, along with franchise creators Ted Elliott and Terry Rossio. Rather than portraying the titular hero, Depp will take on the role of the Lone Ranger's Native American sidekick, Tonto; donning the trademark black mask will be the ironically-handsome Armie Hammer (*The Social Network*), an actor who was born some 23 years after Depp.

The earliest trailers for *The Lone Ranger* suggested an old-timey yarn being "re-booted" as a metal-twisting, action-laden affair; however, clues about the film's underlying sensibility—and Johnny Depp's pivotal contribution thereto—remain in short supply at the time of writing. Will Depp be able to forge yet another of his memorable interpretations from the traditionally subservient Tonto? The talk of Depp's Tonto being a "shamanic" figure was certainly confirmed by production stills in which his face was daubed with black streaks of tribal makeup, with a stuffed crow sitting defiantly atop his cranium.

With high-octane action sequences and dramatic desert panoramas, *The Lone Ranger* promises to be a memorable big-screen revival for the masked lawman and his companion Tonto, played by Depp.

Another early promotional image for *The Lone Ranger* offered the intriguing suggestion that the personal dynamic between the Lone Ranger and Tonto had been given a significant makeover: The image in question showed Armie Hammer gazing heroically into the great West as Johnny Depp scowled at him with unalloyed contempt.

Unusually for him, Depp will follow *The Lone Ranger* by starring in another solidly mainstream venture. According to initial reports, *Transcendence* (the directorial debut of revered cinematographer Wally Pfister) belongs to a breed of metaphysical action flick that was pioneered by *The Matrix* trilogy, and continues to thrive with multiplex mind-benders like *Inception* and *Looper*.

The year 2012 saw Johnny Depp developing his career beyond the parameters of the movie business: In collaboration with publishing giant HarperCollins, he launched his own book imprint, which shares a name, Infinitum Nihil (trans. "there is no infinite"), with the film-production company he founded in 2004 with older sister Christi Dembrowski. Infinitum's first

title is a recently discovered novel by folk-music titan Woody Guthrie; scheduled for publication circa 2015 is Douglas Brinkley's *The Unraveled Tales of Bob Dylan*. Judging by these two offerings, it appears that the precocious counterculture-literate guitar-slinger who escaped from suburban Florida in the early 1980s is consciously reaffirming the core values he laid aside when he stumbled into the acting racket with *Nightmare on Elm Street* in 1984.

Which again raises the question of Depp's apparent desire to maximize his earning potential as he turns 50. The answer could partly involve the fact that, for the last nine years, Depp has been diligently cultivating his film-production outlet. Infinitum Nihil has optioned an intriguing range of material that is suggestive of an actor whose literary sensibility is at once surprisingly refined and highly eclectic. One early acquisition was *Rex Mundi*, a graphic-novel series in which the Inquisition has lasted into the twentieth century, keeping most of Europe under the yoke of the Catholic church. After years of development, Depp's production outfit just recently

relinquished its rights to *Shantaram*, a picaresque yarn that features an escaped Australian convict who ends up assisting the Mujahideen during the Soviet war in Afghanistan.

*Shantaram* is one of the many early Infinitum Nihil projects that failed to reach the production stage. But in 2011 the company boasted its first major project, Martin Scorsese's darkly complex homage to early cinema, *Hugo*; this was followed a year later by Tim Burton's *Dark Shadows*.

Infinitum Nihil's slate of projects in development represents an embarrassment of riches, with Depp's endorsement the only common thread: Most ambitiously, he optioned *In the Hand of Dante*, a powerfully ambitious spiritual opus written by the earthy and esteemed New York novelist Nick Tosches. A slightly more commercial proposition would be the mooted live-action movie about the beloved children's author and illustrator Dr. Seuss (Theodor Geisel). There is also another graphic novel, *The Vault*, plus a proposed re-make of the 1934 comedy crime classic *The Thin Man*; throw in the acclaimed children's book *Attica* along with sundry other coveted titles

and one gets the distinct sense that Infinitum Nihil could ultimately prove to be a hothouse of fresh new ideas—either that, or the grand folly of a well-meaning movie star who can afford to cultivate pet projects as a hip sideline.

Johnny Depp is among the small handful of movie stars who can currently make legitimate claim to primacy in his trade. Yet he is the only member of this elite group who has a chance to reach far higher plateaux: to become the newest member of a pantheon of Hollywood immortals whose membership list was last augmented many years ago. Depp has pulled off so many minor miracles as an actor that it seems almost reasonable to envision his name and likeness enduring for untold decades to come.

Most civilians regard the age of 50 as something of a cautionary road sign—but that is not the kind of thinking that set Johnny Depp on the preposterously convoluted career path by which he reached his current position. It's virtually impossible to imagine this elusive spirit easing his foot off the gas, and steering himself toward the old straight and narrow-minded.

# Filmography

## As Actor

### FEATURE FILMS

*Opening dates are for the US (general release) unless stated.*

**A Nightmare on Elm Street**
(New Line Cinema/Media Home Entertainment/
Smart Egg Pictures/The Elm Street Venture)
91 minutes
Director: Wes Craven
Screenplay: Wes Craven
Cinematography: Jacques Haitkin
Cast: John Saxon (Lt. Donald Thompson), Ronee
Blakley (Marge Thompson), Heather Langenkamp
(Nancy Thompson), Amanda Wyss (Christina "Tina"
Gray), Jsu Garcia (Rod Lane), Johnny Depp (Glen
Lantz), Robert Englund (Fred Krueger)
Opened November 16, 1984

**Private Resort**
(Delphi III Productions/TriStar)
82 minutes
Director: George Bowers
Screenplay: Gordon Mitchell
Cinematography: Adam Greenberg
Cast: Rob Morrow (Ben), Johnny Depp (Jack),
Emily Longstreth (Patti), Karyn O'Bryan (Dana),
Hector Elizondo (The Maestro)
Opened May 3, 1985

**Platoon**
(Hemdale Film/Cinema 86 [uncredited])
120 minutes
Director: Oliver Stone
Screenplay: Oliver Stone
Cinematography: Robert Richardson
Cast: Keith David (King), Forest Whitaker (Big Harold),
Kevin Dillon (Bunny), John C. McGinley (Sgt. O'Neill),
Mark Moses (Lt. Wolfe), Johnny Depp (Lerner),
Willem Dafoe (Sgt. Elias), Charlie Sheen (Chris)
Opened December 24, 1986

**Cry-Baby**
(Universal/Imagine)
85 minutes
Director: John Waters
Screenplay: John Waters
Cinematography: David Insley
Cast: Johnny Depp (Cry-Baby), Amy Locane (Allison
Vernon-Williams), Susan Tyrrell (Ramona Rickettes),
Polly Bergen (Mrs. Vernon-Williams), Iggy Pop
(Belvedere Rickettes), Ricki Lake (Pepper Walker)
Opened April 6, 1990

**Edward Scissorhands**
(Twentieth Century Fox)
105 minutes
Director: Tim Burton
Screenplay: Caroline Thompson
Cinematography: Stefan Czapsky
Cast: Johnny Depp (Edward Scissorhands),
Winona Ryder (Kim), Dianne Wiest (Peg), Anthony
Michael Hall (Jim), Kathy Baker (Joyce),
Vincent Price (The Inventor)
Opened December 14, 1990

**Freddy's Dead: The Final Nightmare**
(New Line Cinema/Nicholas)
89 minutes
105 minutes (original release)
93 minutes (TV version)
Director: Rachel Talalay
Screenplay: Michael De Luca
Cinematography: Declan Quinn
Cast: Robert Englund (Freddy Krueger), Lisa Zane
(Maggie Burroughs), Shon Greenblatt (John Doe),
Lezlie Deane (Tracy), Ricky Dean Logan (Carlos),
Johnny Depp (Guy on TV)
Opened September 13, 1991

**Arizona Dream**
(Canal+/Constellation/Hachette Première/Union
Générale Cinématographique)
142 minutes
119 minutes (DVD version)
Director: Emir Kusturica
Screenplay: David Atkins
Cinematography: Vilko Filac
Cast: Johnny Depp (Axel Blackmar), Jerry Lewis (Leo
Sweetie), Faye Dunaway (Elaine Stalker), Lili Taylor
(Grace Stalker), Vincent Gallo (Paul Leger)
First shown January 6, 1993 (France);
Opened September 9, 1994 in US

**Benny & Joon**
(Metro-Goldwyn-Mayer/Roth-Arnold)
98 minutes
Director: Jeremiah S. Chechik
Screenplay: Barry Berman
Cinematography: John Schwartzman
Cast: Johnny Depp (Sam), Mary Stuart Masterson
(Juniper "Joon" Pearl), Aidan Quinn (Benjamin
"Benny" Pearl), Julianne Moore (Ruthie),
Oliver Platt (Eric)
Opened April 16, 1993

**What's Eating Gilbert Grape**
(Paramount)
118 minutes
Director: Lasse Hallström
Screenplay: Peter Hedges
Cinematography: Sven Nykvist
Cast: Johnny Depp (Gilbert Grape), Leonardo DiCaprio
(Arnie Grape), Juliette Lewis (Becky), Mary Steenburgen
(Betty Carver), Darlene Cates (Bonnie Grape)
Opened March 4, 1994

**Ed Wood**
(Touchstone)
127 minutes
Director: Tim Burton
Screenplay: Scott Alexander, Larry Karaszewski
Cinematography: Stefan Czapsky
Cast: Johnny Depp (Ed Wood), Martin Landau
(Bela Lugosi), Sarah Jessica Parker (Dolores Fuller),
Patricia Arquette (Kathy O'Hara), Bill Murray (Bunny
Breckinridge)
Opened September 28, 1994

**Don Juan DeMarco**
(New Line Cinema/American Zoetrope/Outlaw)
97 minutes
Director: Jeremy Leven
Screenplay: Jeremy Leven
Cinematography: Ralf D. Bode
Cast: Marlon Brando (Dr. Jack Mickler), Johnny Depp
(Don Juan), Faye Dunaway (Marilyn Mickler), Géraldine
Pailhas (Doña Ana), Bob Dishy (Dr. Paul Showalter)
Opened April 7, 1995

**Dead Man**
(Pandora Filmproduktion/JVC Entertainment
Networks/Newmarket Capital Group/
12 Gauge Productions)
121 minutes
Director: Jim Jarmusch
Screenplay: Jim Jarmusch
Cinematography: Robby Müller
Cast: Johnny Depp (William Blake), Gary Farmer
(Nobody), Crispin Glover (Train Fireman),
Robert Mitchum (John Dickinson), Michael Wincott
(Conway Twill), Mili Avital (Thel Russell), John Hurt
(John Scholfield)
First shown May 26, 1995 (Cannes Film Festival);
Opened May 10, 1996 in US

**Nick of Time**
(Paramount)
90 minutes
Director: John Badham
Screenplay: Patrick Sheane Duncan
Cinematography: Roy H. Wagner
Cast: Johnny Depp (Gene Watson), Courtney Chase
(Lynn Watson), Charles S. Dutton (Huey), Christopher
Walken (Mr. Smith), Roma Maffia (Ms. Jones),
Marsha Mason (Gov. Eleanor Grant)
Opened November 22, 1995

**Donnie Brasco**
(Mandalay/Baltimore/Mark Johnson)
127 minutes (147 minutes extended cut)
Director: Mike Newell
Screenplay: Paul Attanasio
Cinematography: Peter Sova
Cast: Al Pacino (Benjamin "Lefty" Ruggiero),
Johnny Depp (Donnie Brasco/Joseph D. "Joe" Pistone),
Michael Madsen (Sonny Black), Bruno Kirby (Nicky),
James Russo (Paulie)
Opened February 28, 1997

**The Brave**
(Jeremy Thomas/Acappella/Brave/Majestic
Films International)
123 minutes
Director: Johnny Depp
Screenplay: Paul McCudden, Johnny Depp, D.P. Depp
Cinematography: Vilko Filac, Eugene D. Shlugleit
Cast: Johnny Depp (Raphael), Marlon Brando
(McCarthy), Marshall Bell (Larry), Elpidia Carrillo
(Rita), Cody Lightning (Frankie)
Opened July 30, 1997 (France); unreleased in US

**Fear and Loathing in Las Vegas**
(Fear and Loathing LLC/Rhino Films/Shark
Productions/Summit Entertainment/Universal)
118 minutes
Director: Terry Gilliam
Screenplay: Terry Gilliam, Tony Grisoni, Tod Davies,
Alex Cox
Cinematography: Nicola Pecorini
Cast: Johnny Depp (Raoul Duke), Benicio Del Toro
(Dr. Gonzo), Tobey Maguire (Hitchhiker),
Ellen Barkin (Waitress at North Star Café), Gary
Busey (Highway Patrolman)
Opened May 22, 1998

**The Ninth Gate**
(Artisan Entertainment/R.P. Productions/Orly Films/
TF1 Films Production/Bac Films/Canal+/Kino Vision/
Origen Producciones Cinematograficas S.A./
Vía Digital)
133 minutes
Director: Roman Polanski
Screenplay: John Brownjohn, Enrique Urbizu,
Roman Polanski
Cinematography: Darius Khondji
Cast: Johnny Depp (Dean Corso), Frank Langella
(Boris Balkan), Lena Olin (Liana Telfer), Emmanuelle
Seigner (The Girl), Barbara Jefford (Baroness Kessler),
Jack Taylor (Victor Fargas)
First shown August 25, 1999 (Belgium/France);
Opened March 10, 2000 in US

**The Astronaut's Wife**
(New Line Cinema/Mad Chance)
109 minutes
Director. Rand Ravich
Screenplay: Rand Ravich
Cinematography: Allen Daviau
Cast: Johnny Depp (Commander Spencer Armacost),
Charlize Theron (Jillian Armacost), Joe Morton
(Sherman Reese, NASA Representative),
Clea DuVall (Nan), Donna Murphy (Natalie Streck),
Nick Cassavetes (Capt. Alex Streck)
Opened August 27, 1999

**Sleepy Hollow**
(Paramount/Mandalay/American Zoetrope/Karol Film
Productions/Tim Burton Productions)
105 minutes
Director: Tim Burton
Screenplay: Andrew Kevin Walker
Cinematography: Emmanuel Lubezki
Cast: Johnny Depp (Ichabod Crane), Christina Ricci
(Katrina Van Tassel), Miranda Richardson (Lady Van
Tassel/Crone), Michael Gambon (Baltus Van Tassel),
Christopher Walken (Hessian Horseman)
Opened November 19, 1999

**The Man Who Cried**
(Studio Canal/Universal/Adventure Pictures/
Working Title Films)
100 minutes
Director: Sally Potter
Screenplay: Sally Potter
Cinematography: Sacha Vierny
Cast: Christina Ricci (Suzie), Oleg Yankovskiy (Father),
Cate Blanchett (Lola), Miriam Karlin (Madame
Goldstein), Johnny Depp (Cesar), John Turturro
(Dante Dominio)
First shown September 2, 2000 (Venice Film Festival);
unreleased in US

**Before Night Falls**
(El Mar Pictures/Grandview Pictures)
133 minutes
Director: Julian Schnabel
Screenplay: Cunningham O'Keefe, Lázaro Gómez
Carriles, Julian Schnabel
Cinematography: Xavier Pérez Grobet, Guillermo
Rosas
Cast: Javier Bardem (Reinaldo Arenas), Johnny Depp
(Bon Bon/Lt. Victor), Olivier Martinez (Lázaro Gómez
Carriles), Andrea Di Stefano (Pepe Malas), Santiago
Magill (Tomas Diego)
First shown September 3, 2000 (Venice Film Festival);
Opened January 26, 2001 in US

**Chocolat**
(Miramax/David Brown Productions/Fat Free)
121 minutes
Director: Lasse Hallström
Screenplay: Robert Nelson Jacobs
Cinematography: Roger Pratt
Cast: Juliette Binoche (Vianne Rocher), Judi Dench
(Amande Voizin), Johnny Depp (Roux), Alfred
Molina (Comte de Reynaud), Carrie-Anne Moss
(Caroline Clairmont)
Opened January 19, 2001

**Blow**
(Apostle/Avery Pix/New Line Cinema/Spanky Pictures)
124 minutes
Director: Ted Demme
Screenplay: David McKenna, Nick Cassavetes
Cinematography: Ellen Kuras
Cast: Johnny Depp (George Jung), Penélope Cruz
(Mirtha Jung), Franka Potente (Barbara Buckley),
Rachel Griffiths (Ermine Jung), Paul Reubens
(Derek Foreal)
Opened April 6, 2001

**From Hell**
(Twentieth Century Fox/Underworld)
122 minutes
Directors: Albert Hughes, Allen Hughes
Screenplay: Terry Hayes, Rafael Yglesias
Cinematography: Peter Deming
Cast: Johnny Depp (Inspector Frederick Abberline),
Heather Graham (Mary Kelly), Ian Holm (Sir William
Gull), Robbie Coltrane (Sergeant Peter Godley),
Ian Richardson (Sir Charles Warren)
Opened October 19, 2001

**Pirates of the Caribbean: The Curse of the
Black Pearl**
(Walt Disney/Jerry Bruckheimer Films)
143 minutes
Director: Gore Verbinski
Screenplay: Ted Elliott, Terry Rossio
Cinematography: Dariusz Wolski
Cast: Johnny Depp (Jack Sparrow), Geoffrey Rush
(Barbossa), Orlando Bloom (Will Turner), Keira
Knightley (Elizabeth Swann), Jack Davenport
(Norrington), Jonathan Pryce (Governor Weatherby
Swann), Lee Arenberg (Pintel), Mackenzie Crook
(Ragetti)
Opened July 9, 2003

**Once Upon a Time in Mexico**
(Columbia/Dimension Films/Troublemaker Studios)
102 minutes
Director: Robert Rodriguez
Screenplay: Robert Rodriguez
Cinematography: Robert Rodriguez
Cast: Antonio Banderas (El Mariachi), Salma Hayek
(Carolina), Johnny Depp (Sands), Mickey Rourke
(Billy), Eva Mendes (Ajedrez)
Opened September 12, 2003

**Secret Window**
(Grand Slam Productions/Columbia/
Pariah Entertainment)
96 minutes
Director: David Koepp
Screenplay: David Koepp
Cinematography: Fred Murphy
Cast: Johnny Depp (Mort Rainey), John Turturro (John
Shooter), Maria Bello (Amy Rainey), Timothy Hutton
(Ted Milner), Charles S. Dutton (Ken Karsch)
Opened March 12, 2004

**Happily Ever After**
(Hirsch/Pathé Renn Productions/TF1 Films
Production/Canal+/Centre National de la
Cinématographie)
100 minutes
Director: Yvan Attal
Screenplay: Yvan Attal
Cinematography: Rémy Chevrin
Cast: Johnny Depp (L'Inconnu), Charlotte Gainsbourg
(Gabrielle), Sébastien Vidal (Thibault), Yvan Attal
(Vincent), Chloé Combret (Chloé)
Opened August 25, 2004 (France); unreleased in US

**Finding Neverland**
(Miramax/FilmColony)
106 minutes
Director: Marc Forster
Screenplay: David Magee
Cinematography: Roberto Schaefer
Cast: Johnny Depp (Sir James Matthew Barrie),
Kate Winslet (Sylvia Llewelyn Davies), Julie Christie
(Mrs. Emma du Maurier), Radha Mitchell (Mary Ansell
Barrie), Dustin Hoffman (Charles Frohman),
Freddie Highmore (Peter Llewelyn Davies), Ian Hart
(Sir Arthur Conan Doyle)
Opened November 24, 2004

**The Libertine**
(The Weinstein Company/Isle of Man Film/Mr. Mudd/
First Choice Films 2004/Odyssey Entertainment)
114 minutes
Director: Laurence Dunmore
Screenplay: Stephen Jeffreys
Cinematography: Alexander Melman
Cast: Johnny Depp (Rochester), John Malkovich
(Charles II), Samantha Morton (Elizabeth Barry),
Rosamund Pike (Elizabeth Malet)
First shown September 16, 2004 (Toronto International
Film Festival);
Opened March 10, 2006 in US

**Charlie and the Chocolate Factory**
(Warner Bros./Village Roadshow Pictures/The Zanuck
Company/Plan B Entertainment/Theobald Film
Productions/Tim Burton Productions)
115 minutes
Director: Tim Burton
Screenplay: John August
Cinematography: Philippe Rousselot
Cast: Johnny Depp (Willy Wonka), Freddie Highmore
(Charlie Bucket), David Kelly (Grandpa Joe),
Helena Bonham Carter (Mrs. Bucket), Noah Taylor
(Mr. Bucket)
Opened July 15, 2005

**Pirates of the Caribbean: Dead Man's Chest**
(Walt Disney/Jerry Bruckheimer Films/
Second Mate Productions)
151 minutes
Director: Gore Verbinski
Screenplay: Ted Elliott, Terry Rossio
Cinematography: Dariusz Wolski
Cast: Johnny Depp (Jack Sparrow), Orlando Bloom
(Will Turner), Keira Knightley (Elizabeth Swann),
Jack Davenport (Norrington), Bill Nighy (Davy Jones),
Jonathan Pryce (Governor Weatherby Swann)
Opened July 7, 2006

**Pirates of the Caribbean: At World's End**
(Walt Disney/Jerry Bruckheimer Films/Second
Mate Productions)
169 minutes
Director: Gore Verbinski
Screenplay: Ted Elliott, Terry Rossio
Cinematography: Dariusz Wolski
Cast: Johnny Depp (Jack Sparrow), Geoffrey Rush
(Barbossa), Orlando Bloom (Will Turner),
Keira Knightley (Elizabeth Swann), Jack Davenport
(Norrington), Bill Nighy (Davy Jones), Jonathan Pryce
(Governor Weatherby Swann)
Opened May 25, 2007

**Sweeney Todd: The Demon Barber of Fleet Street**
(Warner Bros./DreamWorks/Parkes MacDonald
Productions/The Zanuck Company)
116 minutes
Director: Tim Burton
Screenplay: John Logan
Cinematography: Dariusz Wolski
Cast: Johnny Depp (Sweeney Todd), Helena Bonham
Carter (Mrs. Lovett), Alan Rickman (Judge Turpin),
Timothy Spall (Beadle), Sacha Baron Cohen (Pirelli),
Jamie Campbell Bower (Anthony)
Opened December 21, 2007

**The Imaginarium of Doctor Parnassus**
(Infinity Features/Poo Poo Pictures/
Parnassus Productions)
123 minutes
Director: Terry Gilliam
Screenplay: Terry Gilliam, Charles McKeown
Cinematography: Nicola Percorini
Cast: Andrew Garfield (Anton), Christopher Plummer
(Doctor Parnassus), Heath Ledger (Tony), Johnny
Depp (Imaginarium Tony 1), Jude Law (Imaginarium
Tony 2), Colin Farrell (Imaginarium Tony 3),
Lily Cole (Valentina)
First shown May 22, 2009 (Cannes Film Festival);
Opened January 8, 2010 in US

**Public Enemies**
(Universal/Relativity Media/Forward Pass/
Misher Films/Tribeca/Appian Way/Dentsu)
140 minutes
Director: Michael Mann
Screenplay: Ronan Bennett, Michael Mann,
Ann Biderman
Cinematography: Dante Spinotti
Cast: Johnny Depp (John Dillinger), Christian Bale
(Melvin Purvis), Marion Cotillard (Billie Frechette),
Billy Crudup (J. Edgar Hoover), Stephen Dorff
(Homer Van Meter)
Opened July 1, 2009

**Alice in Wonderland**
(Walt Disney/Roth Films/Team Todd/
The Zanuck Company)
108 minutes
Director: Tim Burton
Screenplay: Linda Woolverton
Cinematography: Dariusz Wolski
Cast: Johnny Depp (Mad Hatter), Mia Wasikowska
(Alice Kingsleigh), Helena Bonham Carter (Red
Queen), Anne Hathaway (White Queen), Crispin
Glover (Stayne, Knave of Hearts), Matt Lucas
(Tweedledee/Tweedledum), Michael Sheen (voice of
White Rabbit), Stephen Fry (voice of Cheshire Cat),
Alan Rickman (voice of Blue Caterpillar)
Opened March 5, 2010

**The Tourist**
(GK Films/Spyglass Entertainment/Birnbaum-Barber/
Studio Canal/Cineroma SRL/Peninsula)
103 minutes
Director: Florian Henckel von Donnersmarck
Screenplay: Florian Henckel von Donnersmarck,
Christopher McQuarrie, Julian Fellowes
Cinematography: John Seale
Cast: Johnny Depp (Frank Tupelo), Angelina Jolie
(Elise Clifton-Ward), Paul Bettany (Inspector John
Acheson), Timothy Dalton (Chief Inspector Jones),
Steven Berkoff (Reginald Shaw), Rufus Sewell
(The Englishman)
Opened December 10, 2010

**Pirates of the Caribbean: On Stranger Tides**
(Walt Disney/Jerry Bruckheimer Films/
Moving Picture Company)
136 minutes
Director: Rob Marshall
Screenplay: Ted Elliott, Terry Rossio
Cinematography: Dariusz Wolski
Cast: Johnny Depp (Jack Sparrow), Penélope Cruz
(Angelica Teach), Geoffrey Rush (Barbossa),
Ian McShane (Blackbeard), Kevin McNally
(Joshamee Gibbs), Keith Richards (Captain Teague)
Opened May 20, 2011

**The Rum Diary**
(GK Films/Infinitum Nihil/FilmEngine/
Dark & Stormy Entertainment)
120 minutes
Director: Bruce Robinson
Screenplay: Bruce Robinson
Cinematography: Dariusz Wolski
Cast: Johnny Depp (Kemp), Aaron Eckhart
(Sanderson), Michael Rispoli (Sala), Amber Heard
(Chenault), Richard Jenkins (Lotterman),
Giovanni Ribisi (Moberg)
Opened October 28, 2011

**21 Jump Street**
(Columbia/Metro-Goldwyn-Mayer/Relativity Media/
Original Film/Cannell Studios)
109 minutes
Directors: Phil Lord, Chris Miller
Screenplay: Michael Bacall
Cinematography: Barry Peterson
Cast: Jonah Hill (Schmidt), Channing Tatum (Jenko),
Brie Larson (Molly Tracey), Dave Franco (Eric Molson),
Johnny Depp (Tom Hanson [uncredited])
Opened March 16, 2012

**Dark Shadows**
(Warner Bros./Village Roadshow Pictures/Infinitum
Nihil/GK Films/The Zanuck Company/Dan Curtis
Productions/Tim Burton Productions)
113 minutes
Director: Tim Burton
Screenplay: Seth Grahame-Smith
Cinematography: Bruno Delbonnel
Cast: Johnny Depp (Barnabas Collins), Michelle
Pfeiffer (Elizabeth Collins Stoddard), Helena Bonham
Carter (Dr. Julia Hoffman), Eva Green (Angelique
Bouchard), Jackie Earle Haley (Willie Loomis)
Opened May 11, 2012

**The Lone Ranger**
(Silver Bullet Productions/Jerry Bruckheimer Films/
Blind Wink Productions/Classic Media/Infinitum
Nihil/Walt Disney Studios)
Director: Gore Verbinski
Screenplay: Ted Elliott, Justin Haythe, Terry Rossio
Cinematography: Bojan Bazelli
Cast: Johnny Depp (Tonto), Helena Bonham Carter
(Red), Armie Hammer (John Reid/The Lone Ranger),
Tom Wilkinson (Latham Cole), Ruth Wilson (Rebecca
Reid), James Badge Dale (Dan Reid)
Opening July 3, 2013

## ANIMATED FILMS

**Corpse Bride**
(Warner Bros./Tim Burton Animation Co./Laika
Entertainment/Patalex Productions/Tim Burton
Productions/Will Vinton Studios)
77 minutes
Directors: Tim Burton, Mike Johnson
Screenplay: John August, Caroline Thompson,
Pamela Pettler
Cinematography: Pete Kozachik
Cast: Johnny Depp (voice of Victor Van Dort), Helena
Bonham Carter (voice of Corpse Bride), Emily Watson
(voice of Victoria Everglot), Tracey Ullman (voice of
Nell Van Dort/Hildegarde), Paul Whitehouse (voice
of William Van Dort/Mayhew/Paul The Head Waiter),
Joanna Lumley (voice of Maudeline Everglot), Albert
Finney (voice of Finis Everglot), Richard E. Grant
(voice of Barkis Bittern), Christopher Lee (voice of
Pastor Galswells)
Opened September 23, 2005

**Rango**
(Blind Wink Productions/GK Films/
Nickelodeon Movies)
107 minutes
Director: Gore Verbinski
Screenplay: John Logan, Gore Verbinski,
James Ward Byrkit
Cast: Johnny Depp (voice of Rango/Lars), Isla Fisher
(voice of Beans), Abigail Breslin (voice of Priscilla),
Ned Beatty (voice of Mayor), Alfred Molina (voice
of Roadkill), Bill Nighy (voice of Rattlesnake Jake),
Timothy Olyphant (voice of Spirit of the West)
Opened March 4, 2011

## TV MOVIES

**Slow Burn**
(Castles Burning Productions/MCA Pay Television/
Universal Pay Television)
92 minutes
Director: Matthew Chapman
Screenplay: Matthew Chapman
Cast: Eric Roberts (Jacob Asch), Beverly D'Angelo
(Laine Fleischer), Dennis Lipscomb (Ron McDonald),
Raymond J. Barry (Gerald McMurty), Anne Schedeen
(Mona), Emily Longstreth (Pam Draper), Johnny Depp
(Donnie Fleischer)
First broadcast June 29, 1986

## DOCUMENTARIES

**American Masters**
"The Source: The Story of the Beats and the
Beat Generation"
(Beat Productions/Calliope Films/WNET Channel 13
New York)
88 minutes
Director: Chuck Workman
Screenplay: Chuck Workman
Cast: Johnny Depp (Jack Kerouac), Dennis Hopper
(William S. Burroughs), John Turturro (Allen
Ginsberg), Allen Ginsberg (Himself), Philip Glass
(Himself)
First broadcast May 31, 2000

**American Masters**
"The Doors: When You're Strange"
(Eagle Rock Entertainment/WNET Channel 13)
86 minutes
Director: Tom DiCillo
Screenplay: Tom DiCillo
Cast: Johnny Depp (Narrator), archive footage of
John Densmore, Robby Krieger, Ray Manzarek,
Jim Morrison
First broadcast May 12, 2010

## TV SERIES

**Lady Blue**
"Beasts of Prey"
(MGM/UA Television)
1 episode
Johnny Depp as Lionel Viland
First broadcast October 10, 1985

**Hotel**
"Unfinished Business"
(Aaron Spelling Productions)
1 episode
Johnny Depp as Rob Cameron
First broadcast February 4, 1987

**21 Jump Street**
(Twentieth Century Fox Television/LBS
Communications/Patrick Hasburgh Productions/
Stephen J. Cannell Productions)
80 episodes (1987–1990)
Johnny Depp as Officer Tom Hanson
First broadcast April 12, 1987

**The Fast Show**
"The Last Ever Fast Show"
(BBC)
1 episode
Johnny Depp as customer in suit store
First broadcast December 26, 2000 (UK)

**King of the Hill**
"Hank's Back"
(3 Art Entertainment)
1 episode
Johnny Depp as voice of Yogi Victor
First broadcast May 9, 2004

**SpongeBob SquarePants**
"SpongeBob SquarePants vs. The Big One"
(United Plankton Pictures/Nicktoons Productions)
1 episode
Johnny Depp as voice of Jack Kahuna Laguna
First broadcast April 17, 2009

**Life's Too Short**
(BBC/HBO)
1 episode
Johnny Depp as himself
First broadcast November 17, 2011 (UK)

**Family Guy**
"Lois Comes Out of Her Shell"
(Fuzzy Door/Twentieth Century Fox Television)
1 episode
Johnny Depp as voice of Edward Scissorhands
First broadcast November 25, 2012

## As Producer

### FEATURE FILMS

**Hugo**
(Paramount/GK Films/Infinitum Nihil)
126 minutes
Director: Martin Scorsese
Screenplay: John Logan
Producers: Johnny Depp, Tim Headington, Graham
King, Martin Scorsese
Line producer (Paris): John Bernard
Executive producers: David Crockett, Barbara De
Fina, Christi Dembrowski, Georgia Kacandes, Emma
Tillinger Koskoff, Charles Newirth (uncredited)
Cast: Ben Kingsley (Georges Méliès), Sacha Baron
Cohen (Station Inspector), Asa Butterfield (Hugo
Cabret), Chloë Grace Moretz (Isabelle), Ray Winstone
(Uncle Claude), Emily Mortimer (Lisette),
Christopher Lee (Monsieur Labisse)
Opened November 23, 2011

**The Rum Diary** (see also opposite)
Producers: Christi Dembrowski, Johnny Depp,
Tim Headington, Graham King, Robert Kravis,
Anthony Rhulen
Co-producer: Peter Kohn
Executive producers: A.J. Dix, Patrick McCormick,
Greg Shapiro, William Shively, George Tobia,
Colin Vaines

**Dark Shadows** (see also opposite)
Producers: Christi Dembrowski, Johnny Depp, David
Kennedy, Graham King, Richard D. Zanuck
Co-producer: Katterli Frauenfelder
Associate producer: Derek Frey
Executive producers: Bruce Berman, Nigel Gostelow,
Tim Headington, Chris Lebenzon

## As Director

### TV SHORT

**Stuff**
12 minutes
Director: Johnny Depp
Producer: Gibby Haynes
Cinematography: Bruce Alan Greene
Cast: John Frusciante (Himself), Timothy Leary
(Himself)
First broadcast 1992

### FEATURE FILM

**The Brave** (see also page 283)
Producers: Charles Evans Jr., Carroll Kemp
Co-producer: Diane Batson-Smith
Associate producer: Buck Holland
Executive producer: Jeremy Thomas

# Acknowledgments

Every effort has been made to trace and acknowledge the copyright holders. We apologize in advance for any unintentional omissions and would be pleased, if any such case should arise, to add appropriate acknowledgment in any future edition of the book.

## Picture credits

T: top; B: bottom; R: right; L: left

**Corbis:** 1 (Christophe d'Yvoire/Sygma), 7 (Alessandra Benedetti), 35 (Phillip Saltonstall), 45–46 (Christophe d'Yvoire/Sygma), 47 (Etienne George/Sygma), 48 (Nathalie Eno/Sygma), 49 T (Christophe d'Yvoire/Sygma), 49 B (Nathalie Eno/Sygma), 54 (MGM/Bureau L.A. Collection), 62 (Albert Sanchez/Corbis Outline), 71 (Touchstone/Sunset Boulevard), 88 R (Paramount/Bureau L.A. Collection), 97 (Christophe d'Yvoire/Sygma), 102 (Eric Robert, Stephane Cardinale & Thierry Orban/Sygma), 103 (Christophe d'Yvoire/Sygma), 127 (Aaron Rapoport), 130 (Christophe d'Yvoire/Sygma), 165 (Jérôme de Perlinghi/Corbis Outline), 225 T (Fred Prouser/Reuters), 229 (Daniel Deme/epa), 251 (Jens Kalaene/dpa), 265 (Stephane Cardinale/People Avenue), 288 (Kimimasa Mayama/epa); **Getty Images:** 2 (Vera Anderson/WireImage), 15 L (*New York Daily News*), 16 T (Pool Apesteguy/Benainous/Duclos/Gamma-Rapho), 16 B (Kevin Winter/Time & Life Pictures), 73 (Richard Blansard), 125 (Ron Galella/WireImage), 184 (Vera Anderson/WireImage), 195 B (Jason Bell/*Time Magazine*/Time & Life Pictures), 287 (Imeh Akpanudosen); **Photoshot:** 9 (Armando Gallo/Retna), 12 (Shooting Star/Idols), 13 (Zed Jameson/Idols), 25 (TriStar Pictures/Entertainment Pictures), 27 (Aaron Rapoport/LFI), 43 B (Tammie Arroyo/CPA/LFI), 75 (New Line), 93 R (Mandalay Entertainment/Entertainment Pictures), 144 B (El Mar Pictures/Entertainment Pictures), 271 (Warner Bros.), 281 (Walt Disney); **Kobal:** 10 (Walt Disney), 28 B (Orion), 31 T (Universal), 33 (Universal), 36 (20th Century Fox), 38 (20th Century Fox/Zade Rosenthal), 40–41 (20th Century Fox), 43 T (20th Century Fox), 51–52 (MGM), 55 (MGM), 60–61 L (Paramount), 69 & 70 T (Touchstone), 76 (Zoetrope/New Line/Morton Merrick), 81 (12-Gauge Productions/Pandora), 84 (12-Gauge Productions/Pandora), 85 B (12-Gauge Productions/Pandora), 94–95 (Baltimore Pictures/Mandalay Entertainment), 98–99 (Majestic Films), 108–109 (Universal/Peter Mountain), 111 (Universal/Peter Mountain), 112 T (Universal/Peter Mountain), 116 (Artisan Pics), 118 T & B (Artisan Pics/Peter Mountain), 134 (Paramount/Mandalay/Clive Coote), 137 (Paramount/Mandalay/Clive Coote), 140–141 (Working Title/Studio Canal/Adventure Pic), 144 T (El Mar Pictures/Daniel Daza), 148 (Fat Free Ltd./Miramax), 150–151 (Fat Free Ltd./Miramax), 154 (New Line/Avery Pix), 160–163 (20th Century Fox/Jürgen Vollmer), 167 (Walt Disney), 171–172 (Walt Disney), 174 L (Walt Disney), 177–178 (Miramax/Columbia/Rico Torres), 179 R (Miramax/Columbia/Rico Torres), 182–183 (Columbia TriStar/Jonathan Wenk), 188 (Film Colony), 191–192 L (Film Colony), 194 (Film Colony), 197 (Isle of Man Film/Odyssey), 204–207 (Warner Bros./Peter Mountain), 209 (Walt Disney), 211 T (Walt Disney/Peter Mountain), 211 B (Walt Disney), 212–215 (Walt Disney/Peter Mountain), 216–217 (Walt Disney/Peter Mountain), 219 (Walt Disney/Peter Mountain), 222 (DreamWorks/Warner Bros.), 226 (DreamWorks/ Warner Bros), 232–233 (Parnassus Productions), 234–239 (Forward Pass), 241–242 (Walt Disney), 244–245 (Walt Disney), 248–249 (Studio Canal), 252 (Walt Disney), 255–259 (Walt Disney), 261–262 (Warner Independent Pictures), 266–269 (Warner Bros.), 273 T (Warner Bros.), 274 (Warner Bros.), 276 (Blind); **Photofest:** 14 (Photofest), 30 (Universal), 39 (20th Century Fox/Zade Rosenthal), 41 R (20th Century Fox), 53 (MGM), 58–59 (Paramount/Peter Iovino), 78 (New Line), 83 (Miramax/Christine Parry), 88 L (Paramount), 89 (Paramount), 91 (TriStar), 93 L (TriStar), 105 (Universal), 110 (Universal), 112 B (Universal), 123 R (New Line), 129 (Paramount), 145 (Fine Line Features), 149 (Miramax/David Appleby), 168 (Walt Disney), 179 L (Columbia), 190 (Miramax/Film Colony), 202 (Warner Bros.), 210 B (Buena Vista), 247 (Columbia), 254 (Disney Enterprises Inc./Peter Mountain), 280 (Walt Disney); **Press Association:** 15 R (Antony Jones/UK Press), 113 (Neil Munns/PA Archive), 200 (Mark J. Terrill/AP), 221 (Matt Sayles/AP); **Rex Features:** 17 (KPA/Zuma), 23 (Universal/Everett), 26 (TriStar Pictures/Everett), 42 B (20th Century Fox/Moviestore Collection), 56 (Paramount/Moviestore Collection), 61 R (Paramount/SNAP), 64 (Buena Vista/Everett), 68 (Buena Vista/Everett), 70 B (Buena Vista/SNAP), 92 (Sipa Press), 115 (Artisan Entertainment/Everett), 122 L (New Line/Moviestore Collection), 139 (Universal/Everett), 157 (New Line/Everett), 170 (Walt Disney/Everett), 186 B (Sipa Press), 195 T (Alex Berliner/BEI), 218 (Buena Vista/Everett), 275 (Warner Bros./Everett), 277 (Sipa Press); **akg-images:** 19 (Touchstone/Album), 169 B (Touchstone/Album), 173 (Touchstone/Album), 243 R (Walt Disney/Album), 270 (Warner Bros. Pictures/Album); **Ronald Grant:** 24 T (New Line), 79 (New Line); **Photo12.com:** 24 B (New Line/Archives du 7e Art), 28 T (Orion/Wolf Tracer Archive), 31 B (Universal), 40 L (20th Century Fox), 42 T (20th Century Fox/Archives du 7e Art), 66–67 (Touchstone/Buena Vista/Archives du 7e Art), 77 R (New Line/Archives du 7e Art), 98 (Majestic Films/Archives du 7e Art), 100–101 (Majestic Films/Archives du 7e Art), 123 L (New Line/Archives du 7e Art), 131–133 (Paramount/Archives du 7e Art), 147 (Fat Free/Miramax/Archives du 7e Art), 153 (New Line/DR), 158 (20th Century Fox/Archives du 7e Art/DR), 169 T (Walt Disney/DR), 174–175 (Walt Disney/Archives du 7e Art), 181 (Columbia TriStar/DR), 186 T & 187 (Pathé Renn Productions/Hirsch/Archives du 7e Art), 192–193 (Miramax/Archives du 7e Art), 198–199 (Isle of Man Film/Odyssey/Archives du 7e Art), 201 (Isle of Man Film/Odyssey/Archives du 7e Art), 204 L (Warner Bros./Archives du 7e Art), 216 L (Walt Disney/Archives du 7e Art), 224 (Warner Bros./Archives du 7e Art), 230 (Parnassus Productions/Cinema Collection), 248 L (Studio Canal/CTMG/Archives du 7e Art), 250 (Studio Canal/CTMG/Archives du 7e Art), 263–264 (Warner Independent Pictures/GK Films/Archives du 7e Art), 273 B (Paramount); **Alamy:** 29 (Orion/Pictorial Press), 117 T & B (Artisan Entertainment/A.F. Archive), 121 (New Line/A.F. Archive), 122 R (New Line/A.F. Archive), 124 (New Line/A.F. Archive), 136 (Paramount/A.F. Archive), 143 (El Mar Pictures/A.F. Archive), 156–157 (New Line/A.F. Archive), 175 R (Walt Disney/A.F. Archive), 225 B (Warner Bros./A.F. Archive); **British Film Institute:** 32 (Universal), 66 L (Touchstone/Buena Vista), 82 (12-Gauge Productions/Pandora), 85 T (12-Gauge Productions/Pandora), 106 (Universal), 199 R (Isle of Man Film/Odyssey), 227 (DreamWorks/Warner Bros.); **Mary Evans Picture Library:** 77 L (Rue des Archives/New Line), 86 (Paramount/Rue des Archives), 135 (Paramount/Rue des Archives); **Alpha Press:** 107 (Rose Hartman/Globe Photos), 119 (Angeli); **TopFoto:** 210 T (Walt Disney); **Allstar:** 278 (Walt Disney).

## Sources of quotes by Johnny Depp

Pages 1, 20, 246, 250, 272 in Johnny Depp: *The Unauthorised Biography* by Danny White, Michael O'Mara, 2011; 6 interview with David Aldridge, *Film Review*, 1993; 8, 180 from "Doing It Depp's Way" by Josh Tyrangiel, *Time*, 2004; 13, 25, 46, 53, 65, 70, 74, 98, 101, 102, 110, 116, 146, 150–151, 155, 159, 168, 176, 182, 190 in *Johnny Depp: A Modern Rebel* by Brian J. Robb, Plexus, 2004; 14, 17 in *Johnny Depp: An Illustrated Story* by David Bassom, Hamlyn, 1996; 18, 210 interview with Emily Blunt, http://www.bluntreview.com/reviews/depp.htm; 22 in *Before They Were Famous: In Their Own Words* by Karen Hardy Bystedt, General Publishing Group, 1996; 26, 208 in *Johnny Depp* by Jane Bingham, Raintree, 2005; 29 from interview in *Splice*, 1998; 33 interview with Stephen Rebello, *Movieline*, 1990; 34, 220 from "Johnny Depp Now Finds Himself a Hollywood Heavyweight" by Barry Koltnow, *Orange County Register*, 2004; 37 interview with Kevin Cook, *Playboy*, 1996; 38, 142, 163, 206 in *Johnny Depp: A Kind of Illusion* by Denis Meikle, Reynolds & Hearn, 2004; 41 from "Foreword" by Johnny Depp in *Burton on Burton* by Tim Burton, Faber and Faber, 1995; 43 interview with Bill Zehme, *Rolling Stone*, 1991; 44, 50, 68, 79, 100, 108, 166, 189, 194, 275 in *The Secret World of Johnny Depp* by Nigel Goodall, Blake, 2006; 57, 59 interview with Dan Yakir, *Sky*, 1994; 63, 72 in *Johnny Depp: Movie Top Ten* by Jack Hunter (ed.), Creation, 1999; 80 from interview in *GQ Italia*, 2003; 84 interview with Holly Millea, *Premiere*, 1995; 87 interview with Sean Mitchell, *Newsday*, 1995; 90 interview with Johanna Schneller, *Premiere*, 1995; 93 from "Outsider on the A-List" by Martyn Palmer, *Times*, 1997; 96 interview with Christophe d'Yvoire, *Studio*, 1997; 104 interview with Elizabeth McCracken, *Elle*, 1998; 107 from "The Hellraiser's Apprentice" by Martyn Palmer, *Times*, 1998; 114, 120, 130, 132, 164 interview with Nancy Mills, *New York Daily News*, 1999; 123, 124 http://www.youtube.com/watch?v=rwDqtkGCGho; 128 interview with Chris Nashawaty, *Entertainment Weekly*, 1999; 138, 140 interview with Heather Wadowski, http://interview.johnnydepp-zone2.com/2001_1116FilmThreat.html; 152 interview with Ersie Danou, *Cinema Magazine*, 2001; 161, 185 from interview *Depp Deals Hollywood a Blow* on http://www.talktalk.co.uk/entertainment/film/interview/person/johnny-depp/31; 170, 258 interview with John Scott Lewinski, http://uk.askmen.com/celebs/interview_500/550_johnny-depp-interview.html; 173 interview with Chris Nashawaty, *Entertainment Weekly*, 2003; 196, 198, 201 interview with Patti Smith, *Vanity Fair*, 2011; 203 from "Interview: Johnny Depp" by Steve Head, http://uk.ign.com/articles/2005/07/13/interview-johnny-depp-3; 205 interview with Sean Smith, *Newsweek*, 2005; 216 interview with Rich Cline, http://www.contactmusic.com/interview/johnny-depp-pirates-4; 219 interview with Martyn Palmer, *Mail on Sunday*, 2007; 223 interview with Miles Fielder, *The Big Issue Scotland*, 2008; 227 interview with Mark Salisbury, *Los Angeles Times*, 2008; 228, 235, 231 interview with Charles Hadley-Garcia, *Japan Times*, 2010; 239 interview with John Hiscock, *Telegraph*, 2009; 240, 245 interview with Mark Salisbury, *Telegraph*, 2010; 243 interview with Cal Fussman, *Esquire*, 2010; 253 interview with Steve Weintraub, http://collider.com/johnny-depp-interview-pirates-caribbean-4-on-stranger-tides/74154/; 254 from "Johnny Depp Talks Stranger Tides" by Helen O'Hara, *Empire Online*, 2011; 256 interview with Earl Dittman, *Digital Journal*, 2009; 260 interview with Decca Aitkenhead, *Guardian*, 2011; 262 interview with Robert Chalmers, *GQ*, 2011; 267 interview with Kara Warner, http://www.mtv.com/news/articles/1672481/johnny-depp-dark-shadows.jhtml; 269 from "Hero Complex" by Geoff Boucher, *Los Angeles Times*, 2012; 279 in "Johnny Depp reveals origins of Tonto makeup from 'The Lone Ranger'" by Anthony Breznican, *Entertainment Weekly*, 2012; 288 from "Kerouac, Ginsberg, the Beats and Other Bastards Who Ruined my Life" by Johnny Depp, *Rolling Stone*, 1999.

Opposite: Johnny Depp performs as a guest guitarist at Petty Fest West, a concert celebrating the music of Tom Petty and the Heartbreakers. El Rey Theatre, Los Angeles, November 15, 2012.

Overleaf: At the *Dark Shadows* Japanese premiere, Tokyo, May 2012.

"So much has happened to me in the 20 years since I first sat
down and took that long drag on Kerouac's masterpiece.
I have been a construction laborer, a gas-station attendant,
a bad mechanic, a screen printer, a musician, a telemarketing
phone salesman, an actor, and a tabloid target…
It has been an interesting ride all the way—emotionally
and psychologically taxing."